The Roman Catholic Church

AN ILLUSTRATED HISTORY

EDWARD NORMAN

The Roman Catholic Church

AN ILLUSTRATED HISTORY

UNIVERSITY OF CALIFORNIA PRESS

BERKELEY   LOS ANGELES

Contendite intrare per angustam
portam: quia multi, dico vobis,
quaerent intrare, et non poterunt

LUKE 13:24

FRONTISPIECE Bernini's fountain in the Piazza Navona, Rome (1648–51)
includes the insignia of Pope Innocent X. The triple crown (*triregnum*)
above the keys of heaven is the most familiar identification of the
papal office, a visible reminder of the succession of St Peter.

University of California Press, one of the most
distinguished university presses in the United States,
enriches lives around the world by advancing
scholarship in the humanities, social sciences,
and and natural sciences. Its activities are supported
by the UC Press Foundation and by philanthropic
contributions from individuals and institutions.
For more information, visit www.ucpress.edu.

University of California Press
Berkeley and Los Angeles, California

Published by arrangement with
Thames & Hudson Ltd, London

© 2007 Thames & Hudson Ltd, London

Library of Congress Cataloging-in-Publication Data

Norman, Edward R.
    The Roman Catholic Church : an illustrated history / Edward Norman.
        p.   cm.
    Includes bibliographical references and index.
    Contents: Catholic origins—the separation of East and West—
Medieval panorama—Reformation—Teach all nations—The church
and the modern state—Uncertain frontiers.
    ISBN-13: 978-0-520-25251-6 (cloth : alk. paper)
    1. Catholic Church—History.   I. Title.

BX945.3.N67   2007
282.09—dc22   2006051424

Manufactured in Singapore

15 14 13 12 11 10 09 08 07
10 9 8 7 6 5 4 3 2 1

Designed by Liz Rudderham

Contents

Introduction

There is a tendency for adherents of a religious institution to mistake what are in fact transient moments of development for permanent embodiments of its founding ideals. In reality, institutions adapt the deliverance of their message to changed circumstance, and their histories are characterized by processes of re-interpretation. The Catholic Church is organic: its truths are inseparable from the tradition of believers – unfolding sequences that extend from the apostles' interpretation of the teaching of Christ to the present. It is actually remarkable for its degree of continuity, and this has always been a matter of conscious policy. In March 416, Pope Innocent I wrote: 'Who does not know or observe that the Church order was delivered by Peter, the chief of the apostles, to the Roman Church, and kept until now, and ought to be retained by all?' This sense of continuity seems remarkable only because continuity has disappeared in so many other institutions, and sometimes – usually, in fact – the institutions themselves have vanished. In traditional society an unbroken succession of ideas or practices was valued as a means of touching the past as one might touch the relics of a saint, and so receive the vitality of its message.

The survey that follows does not attempt an inclusive account of the past of the Catholic Church, nor is it 'ecclesiastical history' as conventionally understood. It is an analysis of the Church in the world, of how it related to the moral and political practices of each place in which Christians tried to live their faith, and of ways in which the Church and society, through dialectical exchange, encountered and tried to deal with the aspirations of successive generations. Despite the modern assumption that the privileges sometimes given to the Church by sympathetic political settlements of the past produced serene 'Ages of Faith', this is an account of much conflict. People who truly value their ideals are militant about them: hence conflict in religious ideology and in the relationships of Church and State. An overview

The division of the authority of Christ between the spiritual and the temporal is here represented in the Spanish Chapel of the Dominican Order in the Church of Santa Maria Novella in Florence. Pope and emperor, with their symbols of office, sit side by side, flanked by clergy and lay dignitaries, and surrounded by the people of the world. The sheep beneath their feet signify their joint pastoral responsibility for preserving virtue and order in Christian society. The fresco by Andrea da Firenze dates from 1355.

presents seemingly recurrent occasions of threat to Catholic order, and it has actually been like this from the beginning. 'Unto these men of holy lives was gathered a vast multitude of the elect,' as St Clement, third successor of St Peter in the see of Rome, noted in the year 95 or 96, 'who through many indignities and tortures endured envy and set a fair example among us.' There were, throughout the history of the Church, internal dissensions over doctrine and order, attempts by secular authority to control religious institutions, and external assault by alien powers and ideas.

The Catholic Church is a monarchy, whose King is Christ himself. His Vicar on earth exercises monarchical authority, which in many ages emulated the powers of earthly sovereigns – and today looks strange in a world that has democratized its political structures. Yet it is the papacy that has determined how Catholicism has in large measure developed, and it is the papacy which will be inseparable, because of the nature of the office, from future developments. It is easy, in the writing of Catholic history, to refer to particular policies of Rome as those of individual named popes – and that is done here – but it is as well to remember that in the distant past, as today, pontiffs listen to their advisers, and the policies of Rome may represent the collective wisdom of curial officials. In major issues of doctrine and order the papacy has always consulted with the bishops of the world. There has been, indeed, much repetitive controversy as to the proper extent of collegiality, and this has even prompted schism. The papacy remains, however, the source of Catholic understanding of the mission of the Church, and the means by which doctrine is defined.

The Church has never been static. Nor is this solely due to unavoidable shifts in the encompassing societies of the world. It derives from an internal dynamic as well. Revelation is conceived as progressive – Christ himself used the image of the mustard tree: from the smallest seed it grows into a large tree, different in shape but of the same nature. Doctrinal truths implicit at the foundation of the Church may over time 'Develop' (the word is used technically by theologians) and receive explicit definition centuries after they were first evident to the faithful. The Immaculate Conception is an example: widely believed since the earliest centuries of Christianity but not defined as dogmatic teaching until 1854. Thus was secured as permanent teaching the special position of Mary, 'by a singular grace and privilege of Almighty God', as having been born into the world 'immune from all stain of original sin' in order to be the mother of Christ – the words of definition are those of Pius IX's proclamation.

The survey that follows is not an account of theological ideas and it does not recount, except marginally, the opinions of theologians. It is about the Church in human society. The account would be inauthentic, on the other hand, if it did not recognize that the institutional Church undergoes more or less permanent change. The affairs of religious bodies are conducted by humans, by people living in the societies of their day, and they adapt accordingly. It has been the duty of Catholic leaders, at all times, to see that these adaptations are measured and appropriate – that the division of essentials and inessentials is reasonably calculated. The Church believes that there is a hierarchy of truths, and that some religious ideas are not less true than others, in a given moment of history, but that some are less applicable in the context of the circumstances presented. The result is not as Delphic as it sounds; it means that the Church uses the materials of the world in relation to the strategy of faith.

This account of such a large span of historical development cannot be even in treatment. Some episodes will perhaps seem to have received disproportionate space. This is intentional: details of what may appear rather obscure aspects of events can sometimes illustrate truly important trends, and are featured here in order to provide evidence of long-term shifts of emphasis in the Church's self-understanding. The book begins with a few paragraphs on how Catholics understand the essentials of their Faith. This is, surely, itself essential in understanding something of the manner in which the Church has presented its priorities.

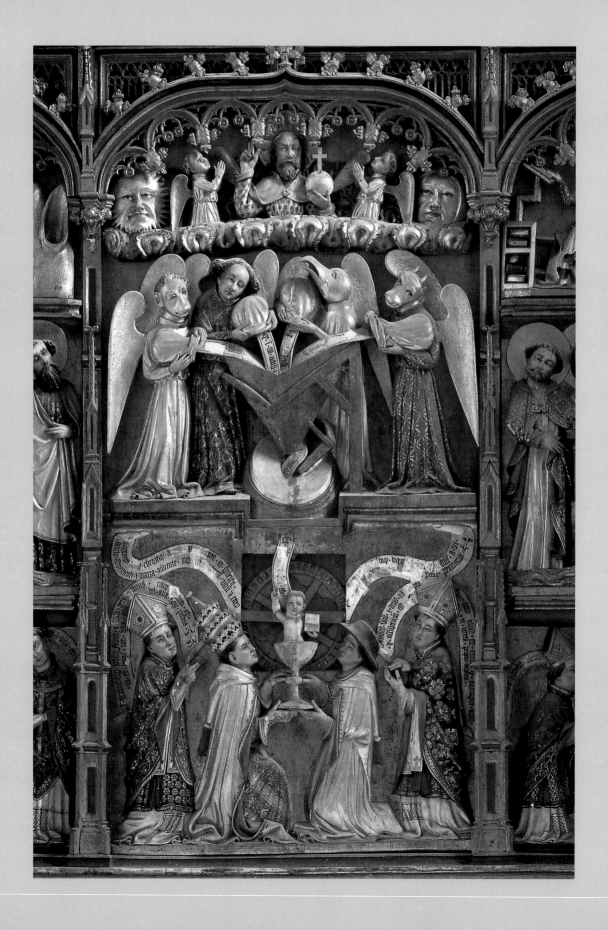

I

Catholic Origins

Late Gothic altarpiece (*Mühlenaltar*, mill altar), St Thomas's Church, Tribsees, Germany. The Four Evangelists stand at the centre of the altarpiece and are pouring the contents of four great bags into a grinder. From left to right: Mark (with the lion's head), Matthew (in angel form), John (eagle's head) and Luke (bull's head). They are grinding quotes from the Gospels (on the white strips) that refer to man's creation from the Word – 'In the beginning was the Word.' Symbolically, the apostles' words undergo a transformation – the four strips become one, and this one strip joins with the figure of the Christ Child in a chalice. The mill, normally used for the manufacture of food, points to the scene's meaning: through the grinding stone the Word becomes flesh, from the grinding stone comes the food of life, and in the grinding stone Christ is sacrificed.

After the Resurrection, Christ commanded his followers to go out into the world and to teach all nations. Catholics believe that just as human sin is universal so is the message of redemption. The word 'Catholic' actually means universal, and the words of Jesus, though originally delivered in the language and imagery of a single people, were immediately transmitted to the understanding of all the societies of the ancient world: they were given universal expression. The disciples duly dispersed to the ends of the known world, to India in the east, to Rome in the west – and perhaps further west, still, to Spain. And their successors moved the frontiers of the faith much further. To be a Christian, Catholics believe, is to be part of that expansive mission as it exists to this day, and to integrate with its purposes. First of those is universality. Christian truth, as St Augustine of Hippo pointed out at the start of the fifth century, in circumstances of great apparent disunity, is what, by definition, is being taught everywhere. To be a Christian is to be part of the original apostolic tradition conveyed to the world by those appointed by Christ himself.

The Church was founded by Jesus himself in his earthly lifetime. Modern interpreters sometimes speak as if Christ was simply a great moral teacher, an itinerant *savant*, a religious reformer. He was certainly all of these things; he was also and supremely, Christians believe, God himself. It was as the divine presence that he set up on earth an institution that transcended the limitations of worldly understanding and yet was first delivered to the fishermen of Galilee. It was Jesus who sent out seventy missioners to declare his message, as the biblical accounts record, and who commissioned twelve men to be his immediate representatives in the campaign for universal salvation. The letters of St Paul, in the New Testament, occasionally employ military symbolism to convey the sense of militancy that this task evoked. It was urgent work, since the lifetime of each person is short and the eternity to which men and women are called is infinite – and the judgement that follows is certain.

Jesus spoke more about this judgement in his parables than about any other aspect of his mission. The great love of God is simple: it provides, on earth, a structure of salvation, a ladder of perfection that individuals in their own strengths could not even begin to ascend, but which, assisted by other believers in time and in eternity, they can. The followers of Christ, the members of his body, the Church, are candidates for immortality; ordinary men and women, and even the little children, as the Lord explicitly said, are raised from the debris of their own collapsed endeavours at self-correction and set upon the way of eternity. The Church is not an assembly of the righteous but of the forgiven, and it was founded by Jesus to be his body in the world: 'I am with you always, even to the end of time.'

So, according to the divine purpose, the body of the Saviour, after his Ascension into heaven, remained with an earthly presence – in the Church he has founded. To this universal body of the believers he entrusted his authority, and also the gifts, or *chrisms*, which were to be the means of transcending differences of culture within the diverse peoples of the earth. Catholics regard themselves as members of that body, and recipients of its graces. They see the Church itself, though an institution whose affairs are conducted by humans, and therefore full of the frailties and corruptions of all things acquainted with human endeavour, as being itself holy. Its authority to declare Christian truth is not dependent upon humans, however, for it comes directly from the God made flesh. The Holy Spirit, the gift of Pentecost, preserves believers in all truth; what the whole body of the believers collectively declare, that is to say, and define within apostolic tradition, is truly the voice of God. Hence the enormous solemnity of the Christian calling, and the supreme responsibility placed upon each successive generation of believers to protect doctrines from corruption. Hence, also, the essential universality: as the body of Christ it is inconceivable that the Church could espouse different versions of the truth in different places. There would always be local variations of custom, and even styles of worship – but these things are not essentials, and anyway celebrate the astonishing diversities to be found among human societies. But for the Church to be truly Christ's body the same simple doctrinal truths must bear witness to his teaching wherever the name of Jesus is to be received. Christians, by definition, therefore, are in communion with one another throughout the world, and when they are not there is, also by definition, irregularity and disorder – and the name of Jesus is dishonoured. The Catholic Church sees itself as that single body.

Tension with the world is an enduring feature of the history of the Church. Christian believers are unavoidably conditioned, by their status as humans, to interpret their faith and their duties in ways that are always scooping up earthly ingredients. It is the eternal witness of the Church, of the body of all believers, which is protected in all truth by the Holy Spirit, not

OPPOSITE Statue of St Peter in St Peter's Basilica, Rome, by Arnolfo di Cambio, *c.*1300. The Apostle, shown seated with his hand raised in blessing and holding the key of heaven, is the most well-known representation of the first Bishop of Rome. Pilgrims still kiss the toe of his extended foot.

individuals or groups or sections among the believers at any time. In Christ there was the most perfect mixture of the human and the divine: if you cannot believe earthly things, Jesus asked his followers, how shall you believe heavenly things? The Christian religion is inherently material since it is expressed in the world. It is only in the representation of material knowledge that the numinous realities of the divine *presence* may be known. In their lives men and women are not admitted to a full disclosure of the divine purposes, but they can know the divine *will*. Through many cultures, and through prophets and sages, it was revealed to humanity from the beginnings of human self-consciousness, and then finally, as Christians believe, in the teachings of Christ. The divine presence was always latent in the world, for the material world was God's creation; the divine will, however, is activist – it calls for human participation and so must be known explicitly. As the Greek philosophers would have put it, the universal requires a particular and concrete expression in order to be recognized. For the God who is a person, that is to say, to be personalized in the world is to be known about; and the Word was made flesh and dwelt among us.

Human weakness, nevertheless, compromises the declaration of truth – and so does putting it into effect within human societies. The treasure is in earthen vessels. St Peter himself denied that he knew Christ, as Christ had himself predicted. Nobody should be shocked to observe how full the history of the Church is with evidences of discreditable behaviour, of frailties of faith, of liability to error. It is probably true that more people have been discouraged from adhering to Christianity by the flawed conduct of Christians than because of any other cause. They are right to be scandalized, but what else could be the case? God does not work by magic, but through the very material world he has created. The Church comprises real human beings, visited by all those weaknesses to be found everywhere in society. What the evidence of their failings and wickedness actually show is how great is the love of God, Christians believe; that he elevates even such as they are themselves. Their salvation lies in their universality, in the single body of the Lord. The teachings he gave have always to be rendered in forms accessible to change over time, and as new things are disclosed in the dynamics of the continuing creative purposes of God. Catholic tradition has always insisted on universal councils of the Church, to discuss change, to preserve essential truths, to condemn error. It was at councils that the doctrinal structure of Christianity was defined between the fourth and the seventh centuries. Thus the mind of Christ was expressed through the consensus of the faithful and announced through the authority of the apostles – still resident in the successors of St Peter, to whom Christ had entrusted the keys of heaven.

Inherent in this procedure for Christian progress was a centralizing tendency. The apostolate was established in Rome, the world's capital when the Church was inaugurated; it was there that the universality of Christian teaching most obviously took its central directive – it was the bishops of Rome who very early on began to receive requests for adjudication on disputed points from other bishops. When the imperial power destroyed Jerusalem in 70 AD, and the Jewish population was dispersed, it was Rome that became, in practice, the most important Christian centre. St Peter and St Paul were both martyred there during the 60s: victims of Nero's persecutions following the burning of the city. The Christian presence in Rome was plainly already sufficiently numerous to be blamed as a credible culprit. After 70, the major episcopal sees (and later patriarchates) of Alexandria, Antioch, and that which remained in Jerusalem, were beginning to lack the authority which the Church of the capital of the empire was achieving. It was a pre-eminence not always conceded

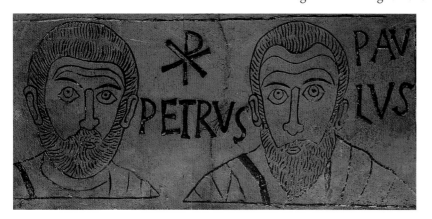

The veneration of SS Peter and Paul, both martyred in Rome in the 60s, greatly assisted the authority of the Holy City in the Christian world. This stone slab, from a sepulchre of the 5th century in the city, is a vivid evocation of their continuity in Catholic tradition.

de jure, but which, by force of circumstance, existed. Matters of doctrinal or disciplinary irregularity, or conflicting practices about the date of Easter, were directed to Rome by other churches in Italy, and gradually from further away. The bishops of Rome were notable for their administrative and theological expertise, especially St Clement, who reigned from 88, and St Pius I, from 141. From the time of Gelasius I, whose reign was from 492 to 496, the bishops of Rome began to be designated 'Vicar of Christ', and the title of pope became established in the sixth century.

The resumption of persecution in 303, during the imperial rule of Diocletian, must inevitably have hindered the evolution of papal pre-eminence in Rome, but the effects seem not to have been long-lasting. With the adhesion of Constantine I to Christianity after his victory over his rival Maxentius at the Battle of Milvian Bridge, outside Rome, in 312, and the declaration of religious toleration in the Edict of Milan, in 313, the bishops of Rome found themselves in a similar relationship to the civil authority as the hierarchies of the classical religions had done. Constantine's religious profession appears to have opaque qualities; although still unbaptized he felt it his duty to adjudicate in matters of heretical Christian doctrine. In 316, he heard the case for orthodoxy against the African Donatists – schismatics who had apostacized during the persecutions – and sustained orthodoxy. In 325, he called the Council of Nicaea to settle the Arian dispute and presided

at the sessions in person. Arianism held that Christ was subordinate to the Father, and so vitiated the doctrine of the Trinity. The removal of the seat of imperial government to Byzantium in 330, and the inauguration of 'New Rome', the reconstructed city of Constantinople, was thus indirectly beneficial to the rise of the papacy: their potential rival in appellate jurisdiction departed from the city. The bishops were left with virtually unrivalled ecclesiastical influence in the western half of the empire.

At the same time, it must be noted, the institution of the Patriarchate of Constantinople created the conditions for the practical evolution of the Greek Church into a separate and distinct spiritual culture. All the bishops of Rome until Victor I, who ascended his throne in 189, were Greek-speaking. Thereafter the Latin west and the Greek east, though still in communion for eight centuries, gradually assumed distinct identities and pressed rival claims – although Rome continued to receive formal but in practice empty obedience from Constantinople. The Roman abandonment of Greek for Latin, incidentally, prompts an interesting perspective on the calls made during the European Reformation, a thousand years later, for the use of the vernacular in ecclesiastical procedures and worship.

The Greek influence in the spread and interpretation of Christianity is not to be underestimated, as it sometimes is today. There is a sense – though not one to be exaggerated – in which Rome gave the mature Catholic Church its organizational structure but Greece gave it consistent teaching and the inheritance of the religion of the ancient world. In modern times it has become usual to assess Christian origins within a mostly Jewish frame of reference. This plainly makes some sense, for there is no doubting that Jesus was firmly within the Jewish religious tradition, and spoke to the expectations and Messianic speculations of the Jews of his day. The Gospels, written after his life, were not intended to furnish biographical materials or a systematic account of his teaching, but to *prove* that he was the anticipated Messiah. Christ delivered his message orally: it was an exhortation to repentance, arranged in the Gospels as a set of evidences that he was the Saviour apparently predicted in the Old Testament prophetic literature.

The Judaism of his day had become Hellenized during the Maccabean period – to such an exent that it provoked a revolt in 168 BC – and although, as the Romans discovered (and respected), the Jews were adept at resisting alien influences, the extent of Greek penetration of Jewish culture, along with all the cultures of the Mediterranean shores, was considerable and advanced. Excavations at the sites of synagogues and domestic dwellings, and the architectural style of the new Temple of Jerusalem built by Herod, just before the time of Christ's ministry, exhibit strong Hellenistic influences. The Greek version of the Hebrew Scriptures, the *Septuagint*, circulated widely among the huge Jewish populations of the cities around the Mediterranean – among whom the first Christian conversions were made. Tensions within these communities, and the extent to which they complicated the relationship between the nascent Christian Churches and the civil authorities, are reflected in the letters of St Paul, himself a thoroughly Hellenized Jew who spoke and wrote in Greek.

The point is that Christian beliefs about the nature of the teaching of Christ became expressed within Greek cultural and intellectual understanding from a very early date. There is evidence that many of the first Churches in the west were set up within Greek-speaking Jewish communities and, doubtless, within the remnants of the older Greek colonies which either co-existed with the Roman cities or were absorbed by them. Since the educated classes of the Roman world spoke Greek, and were well versed in Greek philosophical ideas, and Roman religion was identified with the Greek myths of the gods, it was unavoidable that the Christian message would encounter the pervasive Greek culture and be, to some extent, formed with reference to it, either in its Greek or its Roman versions. Thus early Christian apologists accepted concepts such as the Natural Law and the notion of fundamental human equality, derived from the Roman Stoic writers, and set them within theological interpretations whose ultimate pedigree was as much Greek as it was Judaic. It is not really possible to evaluate the formulations of doctrine arrived at by the early councils of the

OPPOSITE Christ Pantokrator, the Supreme Disposer of all things and judge of the world: a 13th-century mosaic from the great basilica of Hagia Sophia in Constantinople. Many churches both in eastern and western Christendom had comparable depictions of the Saviour in judgement. One hand is calmly raised in blessing while the other rests on the sacred Scriptures. It is a reminder to humanity that the whole world is subject to the divine will.

Church – the Nicene Creed, for example – without recognizing how indebted they are to the subtleties and speculative characteristics of the Greek mind. How else could the doctrine of the Trinity have been constructed? There is nothing in Judaism to suggest it: the God who is One and yet is Three – a thoroughly Greek concept. So, come to that, is the idea of the Incarnation. It was the Greeks whose gods were always visiting the earth in human form, and who, while here, indicated by not always very creditable behaviour that they were really human for the duration of their visitation. The Early Church decisively rejected pagan practices considered immoral, and pagan symbolism regarded as idolatrous. But the minds of the first Christians, and their immediate successors, were formed within what remained an essentially Greek understanding of the world and of the immanence of divine forces.

These considerations need to be borne in mind when seeking to assess the world in which the Catholic Church sought its mission. For the first few centuries it was the heir of the Greek world as much as the Byzantine Church of the east came to be. Here was a single religious realm, transmitting the sacred knowledge of the ancient world, transforming it into

a Christian culture that was the successor to the Roman empire. The Catholic and Byzantine Churches are the last surviving institutions of Antiquity. If you would seek an example of this continuity consider the fate of the colossal seated statue of Zeus, the King of the gods, in his temple at Olympia – one of the wonders of the ancient world. It was the work of the celebrated sculptor Pheidias, and was completed in 435 BC. At the end of the fourth century of the Christian era it was dismantled and removed to Constantinople, and remained there until destroyed by a fire in the city in 475 AD. Now the seated figure of Zeus became the model for the Byzantine representation of Christ *Pantokrator*, serene and stern, seated in judgement on the world. To this day it is the way many Orthodox and Catholic Christians envisage Christ.

The Early Church, and the unfolding history of Catholicism, were formed in considerable measure by monastic tradition. It was in Egypt that the monastic life first began to define ways of separation from the world in order to pursue visions of God's purposes. From the end of the first century, until the Islamic conquest of the seventh, Egypt was a second Holy Land, with pilgrims going down the Nile to Hermopolis, near Thebes, where the Holy Family were by tradition believed to have taken refuge after the flight into Egypt. The country was additionally sanctified by the missionary preaching of St Mark at Alexandria. As everywhere else in the Mediterranean world, Christianity in Egypt existed alongside surviving paganism, and the enduring practice and cultural evidence of the classical Greek-Roman pantheon of the gods. In Egypt, as well, there was of course the religion of the pharaohs – to which the Greeks had looked for an understanding of religious phenomena, supposing, as they did, that the Egyptians had a particular genius for religious knowledge. By the time of the rise of Coptic (Egyptian) Christianity, the traditional religion of the country had also produced the cults of Isis and Serapis, which elicited a huge popular following throughout the Roman world. In this extraordinary religious fertility the Coptic Church represented a golden age for Christianity: now a forgotten world.

Modern rediscovery began with Albert Gayet, an eccentric and energetic French archaeologist, who in several programmes of excavation, begun in 1896, dug up some thousands of early Christian tombs, principally around the Roman city of Antinoöpolis (Antinoë), halfway between Cairo and Luxor. His work would not have found professional endorsement today; he was looking for artefacts from the Coptic past and was scarcely in any sense a scientific enquirer. But his obsessive ransacking of the graves of Christian Egypt revealed the lost world in astonishing detail – and provides instructive evidence about the birth of monasticism. For the Coptic Christians continued the burial customs of traditional Egyptian society; they were buried in the dry sands of the desert, or a tomb below ground, in wrappings that covered their normal best clothing. This usually meant a tunic (colobium) of rich tapestry weave. It is the decorative devices in these – of which 150,000 fragments survive – which provide important information about the Christians of the first five centuries. They show how integrated the early believers were with the culture of the ancient world, with the symbols and myths of classical Greece and Pharaonic Egypt. Here may be seen tapestry depictions of the Greek gods such as Apollo, and Dionysian dancers, mixed up with the lotus flowers of Egypt, and Nile birds, and scenes from the Gospels, vines representing the True Vine, and attributes of the Christian saints. And everywhere there were animals and fruits as pointers to the reality of Paradise. This conventional use of classical symbols to celebrate Christian ideas says more than anything else could about how closely the

Coptic Christians of the Early
Church in Egypt were buried in
their best daily clothes, and it
is from these surviving woven
tapestry fragments that it is
possible to glimpse their world.
Designs and motifs from pagan
classical society are found
alongside Christian symbols.
Here a winged messenger, familiar
in Greek and Roman religious art,
is shown holding a wreath; 5th or
6th century.

Early Church was a continuation, in at any rate domestic detail, of the universal culture of the classical world.

In this context, the spectacular rise of Coptic monasticism represented an indication both of the vitality of the Church in adapting to the material culture and of the rejection of the enduring pagan practices whose tenacity sent the monks into the wilderness in pursuit of purity of vocation. Among the first were St Pachomius, who lived in a monastic cell from 320, and St Antony of Egypt, a layman, as most of the monks were. St Antony was a third-century solitary who inspired all subsequent monastic ideals; he referred to the Lord's words (in St Luke's Gospel, chapter 12) that 'the Kingdom of Heaven is within you', and created out of them a practical and ascetic rule of living which was intended to clarify the essential nature of the divine calling. Antony's life was recorded by St Athanasius in 374, the year after the great monk's death, and emphasizes his asceticism, his many temptations, and his defence of orthodoxy against the Arian heresy. His numerous followers left the towns for the desert; everywhere monastic communities, living under rules, and also many solitary hermits, in effect Christianzed the indigenous Egyptian religious genius. Among the bodies exhumed by Gayet were many monks, identified by their simple cloaks and metal crosses: a proof of the huge numbers who resorted to the houses of the Desert Fathers. Pilgrims came from all over the Mediterranean world to see the monasteries for themselves – just as the Greeks had travelled to

ABOVE St Catherine's Monastery in the Sinai desert owes more to the Roman and Byzantine tradition than it does to the Coptic. It was St Helena, wife of Constantine, who had the first chapel built at the traditional site of the burning bush – where God spoke to Moses – and the Emperor Justinian who in the 6th century began the fortifications. The monastery looks very much today as it did in 1869 when this early photograph was taken.

ABOVE LEFT The monastic cells became extremely numerous in the deserts of Egypt and of Cappadocia, as well as in the Holy Land itself, in the first five centuries of Christianity. Some impression of this is given by this detail from the *Thebaide*, an account of the hermits by the Tuscan Gherardo Starnina early in the 15th century, which shows their cells clustered in a desert landscape.

Egypt to inquire into the religion of the Pharaohs. The fullest account of the Desert Fathers was written at the end of the fourth century by a party of monks from Jerusalem: the *Historia Monarchorum in Aegypto*. It also confirms, as does modern archaeology, the enormous numbers of religious houses in Egypt.

There also came, in the hope of learning about the Desert Fathers, St Basil the Great, a Cappadocian hermit of the fourth century, and his journey is the reason for dwelling upon the Coptic monks so lengthily. For Basil transmitted the monastic ideal to the rest of the Christian world. The Coptic monks were to disappear behind the Islamic curtain, but the Basilian rule, based upon their practices, perpetuated their religious vision to the present time and gave it a central place in the evolving Church of the west.

St Basil was the progenitor of the monasticism of the Byzantine Church. Like the Egyptian monks, he encouraged practical labour and contemplative exercises. The Coptic monks had grown flax and wheat, and had exported it down the Nile to Alexandria; the houses that were founded according to Basilean practice additionally set up hospitals and refuges for the destitute. St Honoratus, who had also gone to see the Coptic monks for himself in 419, established the celebrated monastery on the Iles de Lérins, off the southern coast of Provence (opposite what is today Cannes), a luminous centre of scholarship, passing on the learning of the ancient world to a Christianizing western Europe.

The first monastic houses in the west were autonomous, with numerous variations of practice. It was St Benedict whose work transformed and unified the monasticism of the west. Early in the sixth century he gathered a group of followers to Monte Cassino in Italy, and there composed a Rule that before long became the standard for the monastic vocation of the west. Unlike the Coptic and Basilean rules – both of which were adapted for individual use by the religious communities – Benedictine practice from the beginning assumed universality of application. It was the monastic counterpart of the growing centralization of apostolic authority in the see of Rome. The Benedictines also proved to be the spiritual inspiration of much Christian development in the assimilation of the feudal concepts of government and society which eventually followed the barbarian occupation of the western half of the Roman empire. Some of Benedict's inspiration came directly from Basilean practice; there was, therefore, a clear link between Benedictine monasticism and the Egyptian Desert Fathers. The great monastic libraries that the major houses built up, in both east and west, became of supreme importance in transmitting classical

ABOVE The Benedictine Rule became the standard form of monasticism in the west quite shortly after St Benedict himself had established it early in the 6th century. It is almost impossible to exaggerate the extent to which the Order, and its variants, became the means by which the Church expanded into new territories and consolidated its mission in older areas. A page from St Gregory's *Life of St Benedict* (11th century) shows scenes of the founder's pious acts.

RIGHT An 18th-century engraving of the great monastery at Monte Cassino in Italy; St Benedict's original foundation of 529. The buildings were almost completely destroyed by allied bombardment in 1944, but were rebuilt after the war. The Abbey was reconsecrated by Paul VI in 1964.

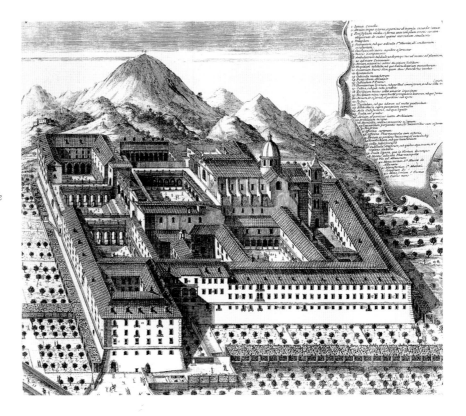

knowledge; it was this preservation of early books and manuscripts, together with the Greek scholarship cultivated by the Islamic schools in the territories conquered from the Byzantine empire, which provided the sources for the cultural 'renaissance' of the twelfth century. In that sense, the monasticism of the west, as in other ways, contributed to the intellectual inheritance of the modern world.

The ascetic impulse within the monastic vocation indicated the recognition that the pursuit of personal sanctity, which had been a leading feature of early Christianity, was easily liable to compromise – not only as a result of the natural effects of the fallen nature of humanity but through the more general acceptance of Christians after Constantine's conversion. The religion simply became less demanding. Believers were originally marked out by their rejection of pagan practices, though they often shared pagan social culture, and by their rejection of the rituals and observances of the surviving cults of the countryside in what was still overwhelmingly a rural society. Most Christian converts were probably urban, but in the towns believers encountered moral hazards too, for urban religion, the ceremonies of the gods of Olympus and their associated divinities, encompassed immoral practices incompatible with Christian ethical understanding. The Church taught the rejection of infanticide, abortion, and numerous sexual exuberances of which St Paul's letters were, so to say, dismissive.

There were, additionally, the pressing spiritual implications of paying homage to the emperor as the greatest priest, *Pontifex Maximus*: this occasioned the martyrdom of many Christians who refused to compromise the exclusivity of submission to Christ by acknowledging the divinity inherent in the imperial office. Many gave up their lives for this reason, especially during the persecutions inaugurated by Diocletian in the third century. The purity of their personal lives characterized Christians, a feature that probably attracted more people to the faith than it repelled. Purity was inseparable from preparation for death and resurrection. There can be little doubt that the faith first attracted many conversions because it was perceived as a resurrection cult – one among many in the ancient world. In this it was, indeed, in competition with cults originating in Egypt that were especially favoured among Roman soldiers. The 'Mystery Religions' also came from the east, and made a direct and simultaneous appeal. It is often supposed today that these cults, of which the followers of Mithras were especially numerous in the army, were successful because of their emotional qualities. To the extent that this was the case it is unlikely that it made the cults immediate rivals to Christianity. For the appeal of the Church was not essentially emotional.

People in the ancient world looked to religion to perform certain services for them; they looked for advice in life-choices from the oracle at the sanctuary or the sacred grove, or they performed ritual sacrifice in order to receive

OPPOSITE An apse in the 'chamber of the millers' in the catacombs of Domitilla in Rome. The catacombs were conventional burial galleries of the sort found in many parts of the Roman world. Early Christians also used them for worship in times of persecution.

the attention of the gods, or they needed to know the secret observances that might secure safe passage to the after-life. These matters concerned the rites of the Greek and Roman religions. To the pagan cults of the countryside, with their origins in fertility festivals, people looked for less cerebral advantages, while still expecting them to come in material form. The secrecy and sexual customs were combined with emotional indulgence. Modern advocates of a female priesthood imagine themselves concerned with enlightened new ideas of the role of women; in the ancient world women priests were extremely numerous, and they were rejected among the Christians (as among the Jews) precisely because they were everywhere associated with the obscene rituals in official classical religion and in the cults.

Christianity did not depend upon emotional appeals, and it was marked out by austerity of living, charitable giving and sexual regularity. Where it was secretive it was a condition imposed by persecution; where it was liable to superstition it merely succumbed to the ordinary frailties of human judgement. To be a Christian meant adhesion to Scripture and the tradition of teaching established by the apostles. There were also many confessions of faith drawn up for use by catechumens (people being instructed prior to baptism). Duties were well defined, especially the care of the sick and distributions to the poor. Where the Mystery Religions guarded their secretive rites in order to exclude non-initiates, Christians celebrated the Eucharist behind closed doors, or in the catacombs, in order to avoid arrest by the civil authorities.

The Christian martyrs themselves must have assisted the faith of very many. There has to be caution, however, because the apologetics produced by adherents of the faith tended to exaggerate the extent to which observers of martyrdoms were themselves moved to conversion. The excruciating manner of death was not inevitably the 'seed-bed' of Christian growth: many believers, presumably most, avoided martyrdom by making the formal cere-monial acts of adherence to the civic religion required annually of citizens and for which a certificate of compliance was issued. For many, this simple procedure can have been no more demanding on the conscience than a modern passport application. The Donatist heresy, which began in fourth-century North Africa, and endured for about the same length of time that Anglicanism has managed to do since the Reformation, was caused pre-cisely by disputes about whether or not it was proper to re-admit to the Church those who lapsed from the faith during times of persecution.

The greatest assistance of the martyrdoms to the growth of the faith, however, probably came not from the deaths themselves but from the accu-mulating cult of the martyrs. The scenes of death and burial of the victims became the places of veneration. This had been the case since the beginning of Christianity. After the Resurrection of Jesus his followers came to say

prayers at the site of the empty tomb – a witness to their faith which the Romans in the time of Hadrian sought to extinguish by constructing a huge concrete platform over the tomb, upon which was raised an enormous statue of Jupiter. This actually had the effect of marking the site permanently, so that when the commissioners of St Helena tore up the concrete in the fourth century – an event witnessed by the historian Eusebius – the tomb of Christ was found at once. The Church of the Holy Sepulchre was built as a canopy over the tomb, and still marks it to this day.

Throughout the empire the same desire to reverence the scenes of martyrdom characterized Christian witness to their faith. Bones and remains interred with secrecy during the times of persecution were removed to churches. Thus in Rome the catacombs south of the city were largely emptied and the bones deposited in city churches; a basilica was constructed over the grave of St Peter. Saints and martyrs interceded for the living, the Church in heaven and on the earth was one and the same: to have some actual, material contact with the remains of the blessed was somehow to communicate with celestial beings. The dead were in a different dimension but in the same eternal existence to which all faithful believers were beckoned by their Saviour. Even objects that came into contact with the body of a saint or martyr acquired his or her sanctity, perhaps after the elapse of centuries. It is this that accounts for the multiplicity of relics that circulated in the Middle Ages. The cult of martyrs, and of saints, did an enormous amount to enhance the significance of shrines and the significance of pilgrimage.

First among such places, after Jerusalem itself, under Islamic control by the seventh century, was Rome. How could it not be so? For here was the imperial city, the centre of the civilized world, the shrine of the Prince of the Apostles. After his confession of faith in Christ at Caesarea Philippi Peter had been named by the Saviour as the rock upon which the Church would be built. It was, following the Resurrection, Peter who was told to feed the flock of Christ. And it was Peter who organized the replacement of Judas, and who was the first of the apostles to perform a miracle; in these acts he seemed to indicate his immediate exercise of the leadership of the Church. Reliable early tradition places his martyrdom at Rome in 64, so consecrating the city, and leaving behind him a Church which, under Constantine, was to be the leader of the Christian world. Even after the removal of the imperial capital to Constantinople in 330 the older city retained its ecclesiastical precedence – though one acknowledged by some of the eastern Churches in only a rather formal sense.

Catholics believe that the Church, as Christ's body on earth, participates in his indefectibility. Secured in essential truth by the Holy Spirit – in the definition of faith and morals – the Church regards the whole people of God as guided by the successors of St Peter. This apostolic tradition is distributed throughout the entire society of the faithful, and it is therefore at general councils that definitions of Christian truth are often determined; it is to the successor of St Peter that the capacity of pronouncing that truth to the world belongs. That is why the pope is called 'Vicar of Christ', for he represents Christ's organic presence in his body of believers. This is a sovereign principle of Catholic ecclesiology. There were conditions in the Early Church that assisted the stages by which papal authority received recognition.

The first was the lead taken by the popes in upholding sound doctrine against the large number of false ideas that persistently visited Christian adherents – existing, as they did, in societies perpetually disturbed by a ferment of speculative religious cults and traditions. There is evidence in the New Testament that these errors, as orthodox believers viewed them, had been present from the beginning. Christ himself had warned about the allure of false prophets, and St Paul wrote against the religious novelties of the times. There were internal disputes about which aspects of Jewish practice should be retained, about the two natures of Christ, human and divine, about the origins of knowledge, and the composition of the spiritual society. The Arians, the Monophysites, the Manichaeans, the Donatists: each in turn lodged within the Church and elicited rebuttal by Catholic orthodoxy, and in each trial of faith the see of Rome remained consistently loyal to apostolic tradition. This not only in itself enhanced the standing of the papacy; it also encouraged appeals to be made to its judgement in disputed points of doctrine.

A distinguished succession of theological apologists added intellectual authority to the resources at the disposal of the papacy, at just that point in its early development when the absence of a centralized teaching office could have fractured the universal witness to a single body of ideas. At the end of

OPPOSITE The martyrdom of St Peter in Rome in 64; tradition holds that he was crucified by hanging from the feet. The site of his death is uncertain, but the tomb of St Peter is located beneath the high altar in the great basilica raised over the place by Constantine. It was rebuilt in the 16th century.

Usually acknowledged as the greatest doctor of the Early Church, St Augustine of Hippo, in the North African Roman provinces, lived between 354 and 430. His most celebrated work was the *City of God*, which appeared in twenty-two books between 416 and 422, and which defended Christianity against the charge that its rejection of the classical divinities had prompted the Sack of Rome in 410. This picture, by Vittore Carpaccio, *c*.1511, is *St Augustine in his Study*, at the Scuola di San Giorgio degli Schiavoni in Venice.

the first century there was St Clement of Rome, third successor to St Peter in the see; in the second century there was St Ignatius of Antioch, St Irenaeus of Lyons and St Justin Martyr; in the third century St Hippolytus; and in the fourth century St Augustine of Hippo, the greatest theologian of the Early Church. From these scholars, and many others, from different parts of the Christian world, the bishops of Rome were able to establish authoritative teaching in a manner, and of a quality, easily able to address the educated opinion of the age. Augustine in particular was the leading advocate of orthodoxy against the Donatists, the Manichaeans (to whom he had himself at one time adhered), and against Pelagianism – the assertion that humans could achieve perfection without the intervention of divine grace. His legacy has extended to modern times, and during the European Reformation of the sixteenth century his writings were cited in authority by scholars on both sides of the religious divide.

The universal position of the papacy was also assisted, in a way rather paradoxically, by the acquisition of the States of the Church, of actual territory given to the successors of St Peter in order to sustain the papacy. The earliest Christians in Italy, as elsewhere, had given money and property for charitable purposes and to make provision for worship. The incidence of persecutions had made these donations insecure, however, and there were occasional confiscations by the imperial authorities. Constantine's Edict of Milan, which in effect made Christianity lawful, removed the difficulty, and the Bishop of Rome, like the leaders of many churches, accumulated endowments and property. Constantine himself gave estates and entire territories to the see of Rome – which eventually came to include the Patrimony of St Peter and the other States of the Church in central Italy, and extensive landholdings in Sicily, France, and elsewhere.

The Donation of Constantine: a 13th-century fresco in the Church of the Quattro Santi, Rome. The Emperor and his successors made numerous grants of land to the Church, both in Italy and elsewhere. Evidence for these, however, lacked documentary bases of the type that later societies came to require for all legal authenticity. The actual Donation document was probably produced, to establish legitimacy, in the 8th century.

The Temporal Power, as it came to be called in later times, existed to protect the independence of the Church in a society where the possession of land was inseparable from political authority. In reality it might have seemed – in a long perspective – that obliging the Vicar of Christ to become involved with worldly government would incline the popes to become unavoidably preoccupied with local issues. In fact, although this happened, and medieval popes were some-times the creations and victims of the Roman nobility, the Temporal Power did also assist papal independence. The nineteenth century, when the papacy lost the States of the Church to the rising forces of political Liberalism in Italy, was also the era that saw one of the most extensive missionary expansions in Catholic history. But there was no correlation between the two phenomena. Indeed, the papacy struggled vehemently to preserve its temporal possessions. They had been legitimately acquired in the first place, and the 'Donation of Constantine', which established primacy over the other ancient patriarchates, and gave the territories of the Church to Silvester I (314–35) and his successors in the see of Rome, though a forgery of the eighth century, actually expressed the realities of development in the fourth.

The forgery of the document was revealed in the fifteenth century; it was, in nature, however, rather like the validity of those relics of the saints and martyrs that acquired sanctity by association – a concept quite alien to the modern mind. The eighth-century document, that is to say, was produced to give tangible verification of what contemporaries believed was anyway true; it illustrated and authenticated gifts of land that had left no other record for later societies which had come to expect them. The rise of papal monarchy, as it happened, exactly corresponded to conditions in the coming feudaliza-tion of western Europe that made territorial independence essential. It was, in that sense, a providential development.

que nous ne dions tout ce que la raison
de ceste oeuure ainsi emprise requiert
Et que nous auons temps a parler du
me. Selon de ce chap' le tristateur
e marcelin au quel il adrece
sa parole et son liure fu selon
rose on briefliure de son orme
te tribun de rome homme sage et prudent
a qui monseigneur saint augustin escript
plusieurs epistres et lui a monseigneur
saint augustin et fu octis en carthaige
par un appelle marine par enne ou
par corruption

Apres ou il dist sont ou cours de ce temps
present Il veult donner a entendre que
la cite de dieu a deux parties dont lune
est appellee militant et lautre eschappe
lee triumphant et que en la fin elle
sera toute triumphant.

Cy commence le premier chapitre
Et ar les deux precedens sont aussi
prologues combien que cestui et le pre
sedent selon aucune ne fuent que un
chapitre.

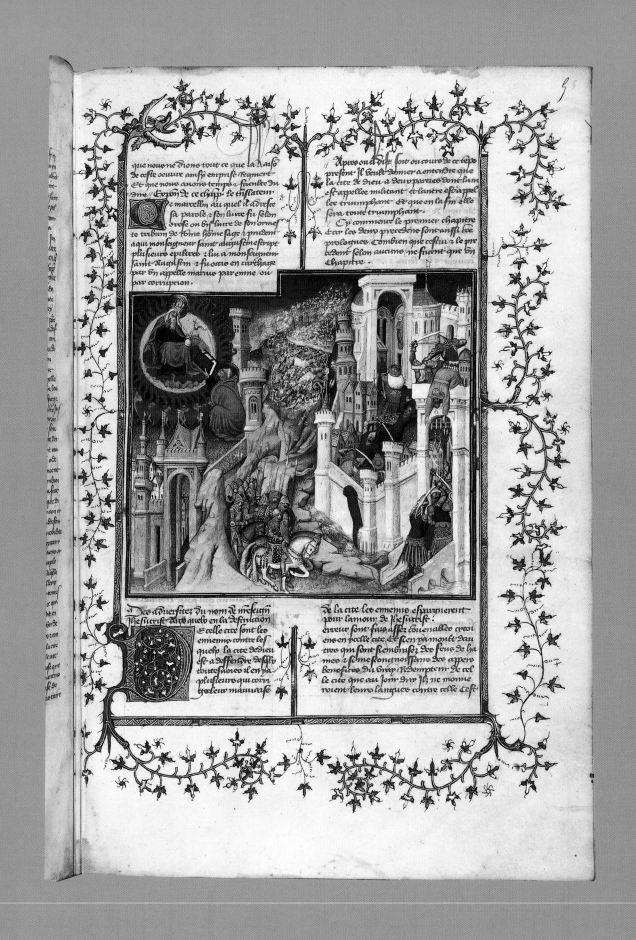

Des aduersitez du nom de nostre seign
Ihesucrist dictz quelz en la desinition
et ceste cite sont les
ennemis contre les
quelz la cite de dieu
est a deffendre desus
toutesuoies il en ha
plusieurs qui uour
bolent mauuaise

de la cite les ennemis espaignerent
pour lamour de Ihesucrist
erreur sont fais assez conuenables troi
ens en vielle cite et scen parmonlt dau
tres qui sont semblables: des feus de la
mes et schnestont noissens des apperts
benefices du brief redemptem de cel
le cite que au soir dur uy Ihesu ne mouue
roient leurs langues contre telle cest

2

The Separation of East and West

Historical accounts of the Catholic Church have not conventionally included the eastern half of Christendom after Constantine's establishment of his new Rome on the Bosphorus in 330. This is understandable, and is in a way realistic. Yet the Christian Church actually remained in formal union for the first thousand years of its existence, despite the persistence of some tenacious heretical schisms, and the sometimes unclear relationship of some of the Churches on the eastern fringes of the empire to the sees either of Rome or of Constantinople. The Great Schism of 1054, when Byzantine Orthodoxy and Latin Catholicism finally severed communion was, however, only the structural recognition of a separation that had happened in reality centuries before. The east was Greek in speech and in its understanding of the relationship of the Church to political society; the west became Latin-speaking and developed an uneasily maintained separation in the spheres considered appropriate to spiritual and to temporal authority. The departure of the seat of imperial government to Constantinople would itself have produced many of the ingredients of this divergence; as it happened, two other portentous events determined the precise manner in which the lines of difference were drawn. They occurred in rapid succession: the Germanic invasions, with the consequent settlement of the western provinces of the empire in the fifth and sixth centuries, and the Islamic conquest of the eastern Mediterranean, North Africa and Spain, in the seventh and eighth.

Alaric sacked Rome in 410 and the 'barbarian' (that is to say, non-Greek speaking) peoples moved into the heartlands of the Roman dominions – the Ostrogoths in Italy, the Franks in Gaul, the Visigoths in Spain, and the Vandals in the African provinces. They were succeeded in other places by other people. They came not to destroy the Roman Empire but to benefit from its wealth and culture. But their political institutions were unlike those of Rome, and their Church, when they were converted to Christianity,

In 410, Alaric entered Rome with his Visigothic army and the citizens fled as he sacked the city. It was a symbolic moment: people at the time understood the fearful events to presage the end of the order they had assumed would last forever. This illustration is from an 11th- or 12th-century manuscript of St Augustine's *City of God* – in whose interpretation the transience of earthly cities is contrasted with the permanence of the celestial order.

tended in places not to be Catholic but Arian. This last feature, especially in Spain, introduced some enduring problems for the existing Catholic bishops. The Germanic legacy was to be the feudalization of western Europe, and, for a time, during the Crusades, an attempt to impose feudal monarchy in the former Byzantine provinces seized back from Islamic control. The original Islamic conquests were in the Middle East, the Holy Land and North Africa in the seventh century, and extended to Spain early in the eighth. The barbarian waves which continued to descend upon the northern surviving provinces of the diminished Byzantine Empire also pressed upon the Islamic world, but Islam proved able to resist them more effectively.

As a consequence of these changes the context of Christendom was suddenly very different: the old heartlands of Christianity had passed under alien governance, and the advance continued until, towards the end of the Middle Ages, the Islamic expansion finally overwhelmed Constantinople itself and reached the gates of Vienna. Egypt, the second Holy Land, was, like the land of Christ's ministry itself, lost. This kind of loss had earlier induced St Augustine to write the *City of God* – and the change he observed with such regret was the barbarian advance on the western provinces. The actual conquest in the east, and in Augustine's own North Africa, elicited an even greater trauma: an Islamic curtain had descended on the world, and this in itself was sufficient to provoke the conditions for the virtually independent evolution of Christianity in the east and in the west.

It should never be forgotten, however, that between these fearful events, and the separation of Orthodoxy and Catholicism in the middle of the eleventh century, Byzantine Christianity had its own institutional and spiritual developments. It is in the nature of Orthodox Christianity that its religious view is much more static than that of Christianity in the west; its changes are subtle, and its sense of continuity with the past pervasive. The religious world of the autocephalous (self-governing) Churches which looked to the leadership of the Patriarch of Constantinople continued to regard itself as one, and the sees which passed behind the Islamic curtain retained the fullness of the faith despite the necessary marginalization of their influence. Recognized, up to a point, as 'people of the Book' by the Moslem rulers, the Orthodox, Copts, Syrian and other Churches were taxed rather than extinguished. Some terrible episodes, nevertheless, accompanied Islamic supremacy, and these were never forgotten – such as the destruction of the tomb of Christ in the Church of the Holy Sepulchre in Jerusalem by the Caliph al-Hakim in the eleventh century. It was the memory of such things that inspired the Crusading ideal in the west. The Byzantine Churches under Islamic control became, through force of circumstance, rather atrophied. Islamic officials in general preferred to govern

For over a thousand years it was Constantinople rather than Rome that appeared to observers outside western Europe to be the centre and principal embodiment of Christianity. This mosaic depiction from S. Vitale in Ravenna shows the 6th-century Byzantine Emperor Justinian I surrounded by members of his court: Church and State in a unified witness to Christ's governance of the world.

subject Christians through their own leaders – which meant the bishops – and this connected religion with civil responsibilities, a link that endured for centuries. Indeed, ultimately it provided the shape of nationalist movements in modern times, in the Balkans, Greece and Cyprus. In Spain, on the other hand, a different pattern emerged: there the Reconquest was by Christian adventurers and kings whose political arrangements were feudal.

The developments derived, let it be noticed again, from conditions that existed while the Christian Church was still united. It was a Christendom in which the see of Rome was still recognized as possessing primacy. How this primacy was exercised was usually a matter of dispute between east and west, and the different liturgical and ecclesiastical uses which they evoked appeared to contemporaries as symptoms of an admitted but lamented divergency. Yet Rome and Constantinople still saw themselves as limbs of the same body. When they were eventually severed it was over the doctrine of the Double Procession of the Holy Spirit. Only an appreciation of the extent to which the Church remained essentially Hellenized in the east, and had become increasingly feudalized in the west, will enable some comprehension of how a question of such precise doctrinal definition – which to the modern mind will seem almost irritatingly obscure – can have mattered so much in 1054.

Educated men in the Early Church, as in society generally, were brought up on Greek learning. This included a knowledge of the main schools of Greek philosophy. St Paul's references to Greek thought are recorded in the New Testament, especially his reflections on the gods of Athens. Since the bishops of Rome were Greek-speaking until the end of the second century it is reasonable to suppose that they, too, were well versed in Greek speculative thought. In both east and west the prevailing philosophical outlook was a Romanized understanding of the Greek Stoic philosophers: ethicism as expounded by Cicero, Seneca and the Roman civil lawyers. With this went a widespread if often imprecise view of classical religion. Whatever particular cult men and women adhered to it was almost inevitable that its expression would be indebted to Greek modes of thought. Classical Greek religion, and the pantheon of the gods of Olympus, was in decline, but its symbols were everywhere and so were the temples and sanctuaries. Public acknowledgement of the civic cults was a duty of citizenship. It was noted in the last chapter that the early councils of the Church were characterized by formulations of doctrine, like the doctrine of the Trinity, which were redolent of the Greek inclination to categorize truth in subtle and exact renditions of meaning. Because of the surviving nature of this aspect of Greek thought in the Church, and because just one such definition of doctrine came to symbolize the division of Byzantine and Latin Christianity, it is worth dwelling, if only briefly, on the Greek inheritance which assisted the formation of the Catholic Church just as much as it did Orthodoxy.

In classical Greek religion there were no doctrines and no structure of theology. Religious truths were expressed through myths, each of which illustrated aspects of human nature: the pantheon of the gods was quite a late development in the Greek view of the world, and the gods had many of the characteristics of mortals. In view of their arbitrary behaviour, it is a consolation to realize that there was, in Greek religion, a practical separation of religious phenomena and morality. The Greeks were also aware of immemorially older divine forces – primordial gods, and the furies (agents of chaos) whose persistence explained the terrifying fate awaiting humans who ignored their awesome powers. Such an understanding of the society of the gods must seem an unpromising foundation for Christianity, with its intimate association of ethical life and individual spiritual formation, and its sense of the unity of God. Greek philosophy sought universal truths, yet the religion of the Greeks was polytheistic – a paradox that the early Christians must have found puzzling. And yet the Greek mind and the Christian revelation actually combined very fruitfully in the Early Church, largely, perhaps, because of the Greek insistence on the value of human social organization. The Greeks humanized politics – and they also humanized religion – eschewing the despotism of rulers, which prevailed in the civilizations of the Middle East, and aspiring to explain the individual worth of human existence.

These characteristics met the Christian concept of personal resurrection. It is clear that the appeal for many Christian converts lay in the exchange for personal immortality of the Greek belief in the afterlife as a limpid existence

The Holy Trinity, by Masaccio, *c.*1427, from the Church of Santa Maria Novella in Florence. The concept of a triune divinity is arguably Greek, and was formulated by the Fathers of the early councils. The Christian liturgical doxology 'as it was in the beginning, is now, and shall always be' was used in classical hymns to Zeus. In 393, the Emperor Theodosius proscribed the pagan religious cults, and many of the Greek shrines were abandoned, but Greek intellectual concepts remained integral to an educated outlook on the world, and early Christian formulations of the Faith show their continuing influence.

of bloodless shades of the dead. The Greeks had sought unity: the appearance of multiplicity in the world of human observation, they believed, was illusory, since the world consisted not of many things but of one. Christianity brought the message of one God. The Greek early Fathers of the Church were soon to establish a doctrine not to be found in Scripture – that this one God is in reality Three Persons, just as the familiar Greek polytheism had rendered the divine in different human-like forms. Classical Greek religion had a strong incarnational tradition, for the gods frequently visited the earth in the appearances of humans or animals, or in the forces of the natural elements.

The Early Church also addressed another issue that joined them to Greek thought. When modern people scrutinize the world they ask how it *works*; but when Greeks beheld the world they asked what it *meant*. The Christian pursuit of meaning was originally thoroughly Greek, and since history, as understood by the Greeks, was interpreted as *enquiry* – it is what is found when the affairs of men are subject to scrutiny – the early Christian Fathers articulated extremely elaborate allegorical explanations. At the beginning of St John's Gospel (a deeply Greek work, employing the Greek device of allowing Christ to convey the meaning of his truth in the images he is represented as using, rather than by recording historical accuracy) there is a reference to *logos*. Now *logos* does not really translate as 'word', but as that which is conveyed in *speech*. The meaning at once has a social dimension, and it is dynamic. Speech, as the Egyptians knew, and as the Greeks learned from them, has creative qualities: it is communication that creates society. Here, then, was the essential congruence of Christian encounter with the Greek world: the problem was how to reconcile the remnants of classical religion with the Judaic exclusivity inherited by Christianity.

The early councils of the Church successfully undertook part of this task. The definitions of doctrine that developed (forced on by the incidence of heretical beliefs) became mixed up with the controverted claims of rival ecclesiastical jurisdictions, in east and in west. Their ultimate incompatibility resulted in the Great Schism of 1054. In this wider perspective the significance of the otherwise rather arcane disputes about the Double Procession of the Holy Spirit begins to assume substance. The Latin Church of the west adopted an interpolation during the ninth and tenth centuries, whereby, in the Nicene creed, the Holy Spirit was acknowledged as proceeding from the Father *and the Son* (*filioque*). Byzantine Christianity rejected the change, on the grounds that there must be a single fount of divinity. The balance of divine revelation within the doctrine of the Holy Trinity, that is to say, was compromised by the change that had been introduced. The traditions of classical Greek religion still hedged Christian understanding: then the altars and sanctuaries of the gods were places of risk and uncertainty; mortals received messages from the gods only after they had correctly recited their proper titles and so acknowledged their powers. In Christian terms the same conditions for entry into the holy presence were still perceived to be in some sense valid. That is why, in 1054, the *filioque* clause in the Nicene creed was so important. In it were heard the last echoes of two thousand years of Greek religious and speculative discourse, and the Christian world divided.

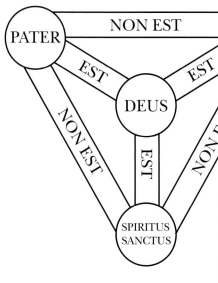

The intricate relationships and attributes of the Trinity were stipulated in the Athanasian Creed, and are required articles of faith in the Catholic, Orthodox and Anglican Churches. Here is a diagrammatic attempt to summarize the doctrine, derived from a 13th-century manuscript.

The occasion of the split was determined by a parallel set of developments in the Church, the rivalries of ecclesiastical jurisdiction. These accumulated in the growth of papal monarchy in the west, with its potential to clash with the rise of the feudal kings. The proximity of the Church in Byzantium to the continuing imperial authority – a closeness of worldly government and the divine purpose that made the Church and the State a single body – produced a quite different world-picture. Issues of jurisdiction became no less ideological than matters of doctrinal definition. For in what was still, after all, an ostensibly united Church, truth was understood by everybody to be committed to apostolic tradition, to the People of God; how the authenticity of this tradition was preserved and guaranteed was of paramount importance. Thus issues which might to later minds seem rather degradingly petty, for being preoccupied with matters of precedence, and so forth, were actually recognized at the time as inseparable from the pure transmission of the Church's essential teachings.

By the eleventh century the eastern and the western provinces of the Church had so grown apart that they were strangers to each other. The effect of the Islamic occupation of so much of what was formerly Christendom had cut the Christian world in two. Contact continued, and emissaries and pilgrims travelled between the two worlds in surprising numbers, but there was no disguising the fact that Christendom no longer existed as a universal reality. The eastern and the western Churches emphasized distinctive rites, liturgical languages, and structures of internal ecclesiastical government. Some three centuries earlier, in 726, the beginning of the iconoclastic controversy had brought the separation into sharper focus: the prohibition of

ABOVE LEFT The Iconoclastic controversy of the 8th and 9th centuries disrupted Orthodox Christianity and also had the effect of further separating the Churches of east and west. The Iconoclast Council of 815 is illustrated in the Theodore Psalter in the British Library.

ABOVE RIGHT The Virgin as *Theotokos*, Mother of God; an apse mosaic from Hagia Sophia in Istanbul, dedicated in 867. Most iconographic representations from the early period were destroyed or plastered over in the various campaigns against them. The ban on icons was lifted in 843.

the holy icons in the eastern Church was condemned in the west by Pope Gregory III. The Council at Nicaea in 787 restored the icons; legates sent by Pope Hadrian I attended the council. By then, however, the virus was in the system: icons were again banned by the Byzantine Emperor – only to be reintroduced in 843. Their significance since that time in Orthodox spirituality has illustrated the differences in religious atmosphere between the two Churches, further creating the conditions that led to the Great Schism.

Another cause of the separation was the northward extension of Orthodoxy. The missions associated with St Cyril and St Methodius in the ninth century planted churches which had vernacular liturgies, and which looked to Constantinople and not to Rome for jurisdiction and guidance. The extent of Rome's jurisdiction was tested in other ways, especially after the Pope and the Patriarch had excommunicated each other in 867. Finally, in the middle of the eleventh century, the objections raised by Patriarch Cerularius to the *filioque* clause in the creed, and the question of unleavened bread in the Eucharist, prompted the dispatch of Cardinal Humbert the Papal Chancellor, and a scholar learned in both the Latin Fathers and Greek texts, to Constantinople with legatine authority. His mission ended in failure. The differences of view over jurisdiction were by then as significant as doctrinal formulations in the creed, and the mutual excommunications of Cerularius and Leo IX followed the Patriarch's refusal to acknowledge the papal claim to be exclusive head of the Church, 'caput et mater ecclesiarum.'

Relations between Latin and Greek Christianity did not cease with the Great Schism of 1054, however, and there were periodic probings of attitudes until Constantinople repudiated the Union of Florence in 1484 and the division was recognized as permanent. In the intervening four centuries differences had been made irreconcilable because of the sack of Constantinople by the Crusaders in 1204, and the imposition of a Latin patriarch upon the Byzantine state. The memory of these events haunted the relations of east and west for centuries. In 1965, Paul VI and the Patriarch Athenagoras finally withdrew the anathemas of 1054: a salutary gesture of good will, but the *de facto* division of the two Churches persists, and they are still not in communion. From 1054 the Catholic Church became Christendom for western Europe – a feudal society with a Catholic version of the imperial identity, indicated in the person of the Holy Roman Emperor.

These centuries also saw the evolution of papal monarchy, a more natural succession to the old empire than any title assumed by one of the descendants of the barbarian chiefs. Romulus Augustus, the last Roman emperor in the west, had abdicated in 476, leaving the Byzantine court as the sole imperial authority. Legalism was preserved; the empire in both east and west had accepted Justinian's *Digest* or codification of Roman law (published in 529), and it was the universalism of its precepts that provided a single sense of legitimate sovereignty in most parts of the disintegrating empire. Even the Germanic kings and their vassals regarded it as possessed of valid application alongside the customary laws that they introduced. Roman citizens living within their domains were left free to appeal to Roman law in matters of immediate concern to them. Indeed, Roman law became one of the seminal influences in the creation of medieval European culture, furnishing the principles of public virtue and order which matured into those concepts of liberty and government that have defined social cohesion.

In the absence of an emperor in the west, of a single accepted embodiment of sovereignty, and with declining respect for the authority of

At the invitation of Pope Damasus 1, St Jerome produced a Latin translation of the Bible towards the end of the 4th century. Known as the Vulgate, it was the only version authorized for use in the Catholic Church until a revision was ordered by the Council of Trent in the 16th century. In this engraving of 1514 by Albrecht Dürer, St Jerome is seen at work in his study. In 386, he settled in Bethlehem, where in a grotto beneath the Church of the Nativity visitors are still shown the chamber in which St Jerome by tradition is thought to have worked on his translation.

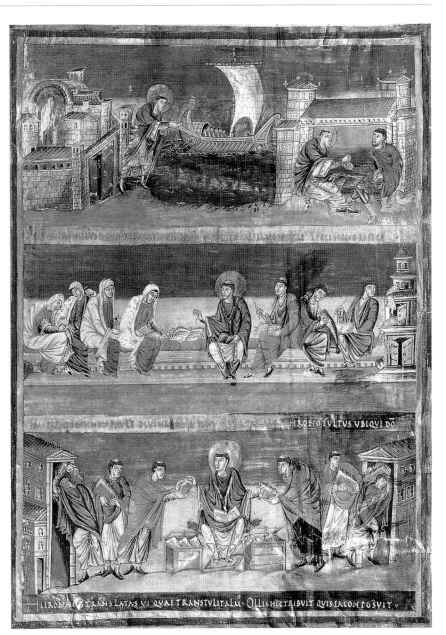

St Jerome translating and distributing the Bible. A manuscript page from the First Bible of Charles the Bold, Tours, *c*.846.

the emperor in Constantinople, it was the papacy, possessed of great territories in Italy, that filled the gap. Eventually it was the popes, too, who came to legitimize the temporal sovereignty of the feudal kings. In the fourth century the Emperor Gratian had declined the title *Pontifex Maximus*: in the fifth century the popes, in effect, took it up. Early in that century Leo I had claimed that he was 'primate of all bishops'. When Pope Damasus I, in the fourth century, asked St Jerome to produce a Latin text of the Scriptures he provided the papacy with a resource for unifying the western Church around a distinctly western language, and thereby also assisted papal claims to a general authority in the west.

In addition to these assumptions of supremacy in the Church, the papacy also sought to become the disposer of political supremacy. The incoherence of the concept of 'the state', after the barbarian incursions, was to be overcome, at least in part, by the initiatives devised by successive popes in legitimizing the thrones of the newcomers. In 739, Pope Gregory III appealed to the head of the Frankish Carolingian dynasty, Charles Martel, to defend the Church. In 800, it was Leo III who placed the imperial crown upon the head of Charlemagne – although he was careful to ensure that the bestowal of this symbol of continuity with the Roman past was in fact purely *ad hominem*, and not an attempt to sacralize the Frankish dynasty. When in 962 Pope John XII made Otto I Holy Roman Emperor, however, a serious attempt was made to revive the fullness of imperial political legitimacy. Implicit in the religious basis to the coronation of kings was the assumption by the papacy of authority to give and to withhold temporal authority. Gregory I had, at the end of the sixth century, emphasized the Christian character of the state, and had achieved extraordinary success in securing the defence of Italy against Lombard invasions precisely by declaring the ideal of Christian universality. It was he, also, who first assumed quasi-political power in the government of the territories in central Italy. A great theme in European history – and later in world history – was already opening up: the relationship of the spiritual and the temporal power.

OPPOSITE LEFT Pope Leo III's coronation of Charlemagne at St Peter's in Rome in 800 was not an attempt to endow the Frankish dynasty with a permanent imperial authority but a symbolical demonstration of the continuity of ancient Roman identity, within a political dignity which the papacy had the capacity to bestow.

OPPOSITE RIGHT When Otto I was raised to the dignity of the imperial title by Pope John XII in 962, the process of sacralizing the office was enhanced. In this ivory panel of *c*.968 from Magdeburg Cathedral, the Emperor is seen as patron of the Church of St Maurice, which he had founded as a royal proprietory church, in the feudal manner, and, by implication, a protector of the Church in general.

OPPOSITE BELOW Reliquary bust of Charlemagne from the 14th century. By that time the historical authority of the Holy Roman Empire had developed, and the Emperor is represented in richly decorated splendour, the guardian of Christendom – and emancipated from the claims of the Byzantine Emperor in Constantinople.

RIGHT Pope Gregory I – Gregory the Great – was the 6th-century pontiff who first governed the States of the Church in Italy in the manner of a political sovereign. He was also notable for enlisting temporal rulers in the defence of the Church, and for missionary enterprise. It was Gregory, here seen in a 10th-century ivory (with the Holy Spirit whispering in his ear) who in 597 sent the Benedictine monk Augustine to evangelize the English.

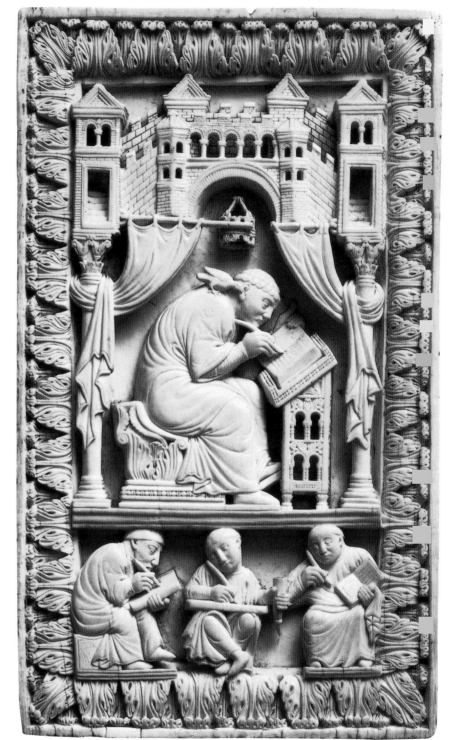

Pope Galasius, at the end of the fifth century, in several writings (not all of them of undisputed authorship) urged the interdependence of the 'Two Swords'. In this understanding, God had granted that humanity was to be governed by the authority given both to the spiritual and to the temporal powers, each to exercise it in its own legitimate sphere. In reality, of course, 'Galasian dualism' led to as many conflicts of interest between the spiritual and the temporal as it did to mutual accord and cooperation. But the image was a lasting one in European development; a kind of spiritual gold standard against which the legitimacy of sovereignty came to be tested.

It was decisively different from the practice of the ancient world, in which the civil and religious authorities were customarily united: the Egyptian polity was a species of theocracy; the gods were accorded civic honour in the Greek *polis*; the Roman emperor was *Pontifex Maximus*; in both Greece and Rome the priests were civic functionaries. Nor was the Gelasian formula a kind of proto-secularization of civil authority, for the concept of the secular had not yet made its appearance. The separation of the spiritual and the temporal powers recognized a single divine vocation in the king and in the pope, yet insisted on a separation of spheres for its legitimate use. The king was elevated by the consecration of the Church; the head of the Church could be seen to have given legitimacy to political authority. What the Church had conveyed it could, in papal theory, withdraw. Dragons' teeth were sown when popes and monarchs ventured upon a relationship which, nevertheless, was to become a hallmark of western Christendom. And despite the later conflicts, and the divisive effects of the 'Investiture Controversy' in the eleventh and twelfth centuries, in general the distinction of the spiritual and the temporal was well matched to accommodate the realities of feudal society.

The appearance of the Pseudo-Isidorian Decretals (the 'False Decretals') in the ninth century gave evidently authoritative endorsement to the centralization of the papacy, in its territorial claims, and to the freedom of the Church from political influence in Italy. This collection of canon-law statements was probably made in France around 850, and included the Donation of Constantine. The documents were not authentic. At the time it must have seemed as if they simply reinforced the balance posited in the Galasian formula. By the eleventh century, however, the Decretals were used to extend the authority of the papacy over the independence of rulers. Changes in the nature of government and society had by then introduced complications in a division of authorities appropriate only to a world that was slipping away.

Roman imperial authority in its classic form was exercised in such a way as to signify a universal rule of law, with a homogenous concept of citizenship and defined rights specified for men in their civic capacities. Many subject peoples existed in a condition of indirect rule at the local level – for example, the Jews in Judea and Galilee. The barbarian invaders of the

As a substantial landowner, the medieval Church was unavoidably caught up in the nexus of relationships that constituted feudal society and its social and economic obligations. From the nobles to the lower vassals, individual homage sealed the relationships – which came to involve church officials as well. Here a vassal pays feudal homage.

empire accepted some aspects of Roman political genius, especially elements of Roman law. But the notion of universal rights, and of a common humanity, found in the compilations of Cicero, and justified by reference to his writings, were generally in conflict with the Germanic practice of local customary law and, most importantly, of what became feudal practice.

Feudalism was never as coherent a 'system' as it may sometimes have seemed to later observers, and there were numerous variations among the different groups of tribes who settled in the empire. They nearly all, however, came to envisage society as a nexus of local relationships, between lords and vassals, which themselves constituted a hierarchy of loyalties distinguished by rights exercised through the performance of duties. It was a species of protection racket, and at the top was the sovereign, the feudal monarch and his court – a grand version, in effect, of the local courts which regulated feudal obligations. Germanic insistence on the laws of the tribe was directly contrary to the universality explicit in Roman Law, and for that reason, and because feudalism was based in a complex series of land settlements, the arrangements which established themselves across western Europe became deeply rural in character and effect – in contrast to the urban nature of Roman rule.

The Church had acquired enormous landed wealth ever since the Constantinian gifts, and was, therefore, unavoidably incorporated into feudal landed relationships. Bishops and abbots had their own vassals, and were in turn responsible for the provision of services to secular lords, despite certain exemptions secured by ecclesiastical law. The wealth

Periodic reform has been a permanent feature in the history of the Church, and many of its most vibrant sequences of development have been associated with monastic foundations. The Benedictine house at Cluny in Burgundy, established in 910, set an example of reformed discipline which many others followed. This view shows the surviving south transept of the 11th-century church. Most of the other monastic buildings here were destroyed during the French Revolution.

derived from their estates was received through economic relationships which were inherently feudal in point of custom and social effect. The result was the feudalization of the Church.

The original Church of the west had been urban; its sees were founded in Roman cities, and it drew its life from the urban culture that both Greece and Rome had identified with civilized living. It was the *pagani* who dwelt in the countryside. With the end of the empire, the Church increasingly found itself in a society defined in terms of rural custom, presided over by an hereditary hierarchy of landed magnates, complicated by the relationships built up through subinfeudation, the inner workings of the feudal system, and ruled by a king who was in reality a chief feudal magnate. Seemingly unavoidably, the Latin Church began to conceive its mission in terms of the same feudal relationships. Christ was represented in glass and mural as a great feudal ruler, seated upon a throne, receiving the homage of his earthly vassals. Popes at the centre tried to insist on resistance to claims by the feudal lords to rights of patronage over religious institutions that they had themselves built or funded. Europe became covered with the pattern of small rural parishes that are still familiar today, with territorial episcopal supervision usually still exercised from ancient Roman cities. Where there had never been a Roman imperial presence, as in Ireland, the Christian Church, when planted by missionaries, was monastic rather than secular in organization – but it was still rural. Here was another great difference in the development of east and west, for until the Crusaders imposed feudalism, for a time, on the territories of the Islamic or Byzantine rulers they seized, the east had not known feudalism. Its ecclesiastical polity had continued to assume the existence of a society, despite its diversities, whose relationships reflected imperial, not feudal, organization.

It was the vitality of monasticism that contributed so greatly to the cohesion of the Catholic Church. The Rule of St Benedict exhibited some variations as it developed: what is called the 'Rule', in fact, was almost certainly a compilation made by others but founded on his teaching. It was a prescription for practical spiritual formation, well suited to become, as it did, the engine of the Church's advance. Monasticism also indicated another *de facto* divergence of east and west, since the earlier monasticism of the east always remained Basilean. In both there were – as is the way with human institutions that aspire to sanctity – periods of accommodation to the world, of relaxation in the observance of disciplined living. Then there were fresh waves of hermits spreading out into the desert places, and new foundations, and re-foundations, by those searching for the purity of the original vision. Hence, for example, the establishment of the great house of Cluny, in Burgundy, set up in 910 by Duke William of Aquitaine. Very many monasteries in Italy and France copied its reforms.

At times when the papacy fell into disrepute – when it became subject to the ambitions of the local aristocracy of Rome – it was monasticism that illuminated the Church's mission. In the tenth century, in particular, the popes became inseparable from factional interests among the Roman nobles; in the eleventh century there were, following the disputed election of Benedict IX in 1032, three popes for a short time. This disagreeable situation (which furnished anti-papal polemics for centuries) was ended by the intervention of Henry III, the German emperor. In some ways monasticism, though always subject to papal regulation, supplied a kind of parallel Church, a standard of purity; it was also ideally suited, with its disciplined adherents, to bring Christianity to the newly converted lands of the north and north-east of Europe. The popes sometimes took the initiative. It was Gregory the Great who had sent the Benedictine monk Augustine to re-establish and Catholicize the Christian communities that had managed to survive the pagan invasions of England. His mission began in 597; among his first works was to found a Benedictine house at Canterbury.

The Celtic Church was almost wholly monastic, and it was to take a significant part in the preservation and dissemination of the learning of the early Fathers of the Church, throughout western Europe. The first missionary in Ireland was St Palladius, around 421, and he was succeeded by St Patrick shortly afterwards. There were no Roman towns in Ireland to determine the organizational structure of the Church, and there were no martyrdoms in the process of conversion – so there were no shrines sanctified by the blood of the earliest saints. Converted petty-kings (of whom there were some three hundred) sometimes donated their homesteads, the *raths* still familiar in the Irish countryside, to the

The Irish monastic craftsmen produced works of astonishing artistic accomplishment, in a late La Tène style. The so-called *Shrine of St Patrick's Bell* was made in the 12th century. The precious metals used by the craftsmen attracted Viking plundering at many Irish monastic foundations.

Monks and hermits sought to reproduce the conditions of the eastern deserts in their pursuit of places to establish the religious life. The Celtic monks who settled at Illauntannig in Co. Kerry, in Ireland, built their dry-stone cells and chapel within a low enclosing wall – perhaps in the 7th or 8th centuries. These *raths* (or *cashels*) were the usual form of the Irish monastic buildings of that time.

Christian missionaries, and these became the first monastic settlements. Sometimes the monks built their own enclosures of circular earthworks to contain their oratories and cells. These occasionally grew to enormous size, with the huts and workshops of the monks accumulating outside the enclosing walls. Once supposed to be merely pious exaggerations, the large scale of some of the monasteries can now be verified through the techniques of aerial photography: at Clonard, in Co. Meath, for example, early claims, made in the chronicles, of three thousand monks are entirely credible. The abbots were bishops, and the monasteries were clustered in *paruchia* or *familia*. In 1110, at the Synod of Cashel, the Irish Church was rearranged into provinces, according to conventional Roman discipline – a change reinforced by the Anglo-Norman introduction of the European religious orders later in the twelfth century.

In its most vibrant years, the Celtic Church had produced schools and centres of learning – at Clonmacnois, for example, in Co. Offaly, a monastic house was founded in 544 by St Ciarán. It was one of several Irish monastic centres that dispatched missionaries to Britain and Europe. The seventh

The great monastery of St Gall (in modern Switzerland) was established around 719 – almost a century after the death of St Gall himself. He was a missionary follower of the Irish St Columbanus, but the links between Irish monasticism and the monastery of St Gall were, at least in its origins, tenuous. The celebrated library at St Gall did come to accumulate an important collection of texts made by Irish copyists, however. The illustration shows a plan for the monastery, never carried out, based on 9th-century designs.

century saw the most vigorous of the Irish missions in Germanic lands and in Italy. The Irish monks seem to have been largely schoolteachers and copyists, however; the Irish Celtic Church produced no single great scholar, like St Isidore of Seville, for example. From the south, meanwhile, learning was spread from the great monastery on the Iles de Lérins, founded in the fifth century by St Honoratus. Irish monks in the tradition of St Columbanus inspired St Gall (in modern Switzerland) in the eighth century; its famous library became a resort of scholars from throughout Christendom. Irish missionaries, and especially St Columba, conveyed Celtic Christianity to the populations of Scotland in the sixth century, and from the house he founded at Iona Aidan travelled to Northumberland to bring the Christian message to the north of England. The Anglo-Saxon Church, once regularized in Roman uses at the Synod of Whitby, in 664, dispatched its own missionaries to Europe: Wilfrid, Willibrord and Boniface. The growing wealth of the Celtic and Saxon Churches produced two notable consequences: an inclination to worldliness, which itself prompted reform movements, and an attraction to external plunderers. The Viking raids began at the end of the

eighth century. It should be added, however, that before the Vikings started
to pillage the monastic wealth the monks had already offered an example in
the same enterprise themselves.

Long before the formal separation of Latin and Greek Christianity in the
eleventh century they had, in practice, become different. They had already
cultivated what later characterized them – different spiritualities. Their very
places of worship disclose the difference: in the east the Byzantine domed
church, in the west the Romanesque and then the Gothic church. Nearly
every church in the Byzantine world followed the shape and theological
purpose of Justinian's great Church of Hagia Sophia in Constantinople.
Their typical decorative and structural features can be seen everywhere in
the Orthodox world. Within the sacred space enclosed by the dome the celestial society calmly descends to the earth. In the height of the dome Christ
Pantokrator, the Supreme Disposer of all things, the ruler of the world, looks
down in judgement. Beneath him, also in mosaic or fresco, are the apostles,
serene witnesses to the materializing truth – and, beneath them, the saints
as guardians of the traditions of sanctity. In the eastern apse is a depiction of
the great mother of God, the *Theotokos*, forever interceding on behalf of the
faithful. The iconography is fixed and sober; in a sacred space the world
itself is irradiated with the divine essence, as the very matter of the creation
is consecrated by the presence of God among men.

Gothic churches in the west, which began to be built after the Great Schism (though not immediately related to it), had a quite different purpose. They aspired to height: the lofty naves reaching up to soaring pinnacles, with towers and spires pointing to the heavens – like the obelisks of ancient Egypt. A Gothic church is a turning away from the world and its corruptions. The heavenly society does not visit the earth and suffuse the material world with the divine truth, as in the Byzantine vision, but humans transcend the world and glimpse heaven through stone foliage, mysteriously removed from the ambiguities of life on earth.

In just the same way, the truths of the faith, in Orthodoxy, were committed to liturgy, so that it was not possible to change the form of worship without changing the truth that it conveyed. In Catholicism the truth was committed to a tradition of scholarly teaching. The truth, that is to say, was committed to a body of believers who developed *ideas*: learning adapted the truth in the dynamic cultural exchange that characterizes the passage of time. Sanctification derives from integration with the body of the believers, and although worship involves a teaching office, the *lex orandi*, it is not its main repository of apostolic truth. For Christ is believed to be intrinsically present in his Church; the teaching of the faithful, when expressed in a consensus interpreted for the world by the successors of St Peter, is the word of God himself. East and west therefore developed different emphases in their conveyance of Christianity. They always remained united, however, and still are, in adhesion to the essential teachings of Christianity.

Bourges Cathedral in France, built in the 13th century. The Gothic style is here seen at its most dramatic: the piers reach to 17.5 metres (56 feet) in height; soaring pointers to spiritual truths which transcend earthly space.

super infernū ⁊ coutustat̄ ē valde ⁊
laxate sunt ōs aie q̄ erant ī iferno ⁊
clamalāt voce magna dic̄tes vñ
dicimus te xp̄e fili di inun q̄ dignat̄

es nob̄ refugēu̅ tair h̄ diei ⁊ h̄ noc
tis quam totun tēm̄p q̄ uuimus
cr̄ tñ. vi ergo q̄ tucbo duit die dc̄m̄
q̄u npi hc̄vīt p̄tē cū sc̄is ī sc̄ā sc̄loȳ.

3
Medieval Panorama

Because so many of the tensions of medieval Christian society in the west derived from disputes between the papacy and the secular rulers – and have formed the basis of much subsequent historical commentary – it is easy to express the Catholic developments of the epoch in terms of political conflict. Such a procedure imposes modern concepts upon the past, however. The disputes were about differences in the balance of authority and jurisdiction within what contemporaries believed was a single Christian order. They were about spiritualities and temporalities, *sacerdotium* and *imperium*: two contrasted centres of a power which was nevertheless universally understood to have been given by the same divine sovereign for the same divine purpose. The notion of the 'secular', except to the extent that it means *lay*, or, in the case of the clergy, being in the world rather than in the cloisters, was absent.

The whole of society and the entire operations of Church and civil government were conceived as representing the unitary purposes of God; the world should be accepted, when properly ordered, as a reflection of the heavenly society to which its people were called. It is not accidental that both the shape of institutions, and religious iconography, mirrored the feudal court, since salvation appeared to be made visible to humanity through the performance of obligations, and adhesion to loyalties, in a social hierarchy. The old ideal of Galasian dualism persisted: God had given authority to both pope and king and the differences between them were not elicited because the feudal monarchies conceived themselves as being somehow more secular, or the pope more religious, but because men at the time could not agree about the boundaries of jurisdiction. When popes claimed supervening sovereignty – *plenitudo potestatis* – it was always resisted by some in the lay world, and sometimes within the clerical one too. It was the right balance that was sought.

A medieval king at his anointing and coronation, from an early 14th-century manuscript, probably French. The ceremonial clearly indicates the separate but interdependent functions of sovereign and priest: it is the bishops who officiate, and who give the king the symbols of government.

Medieval society in the west was, compared with the eastern half of Christendom – in what was left of the Byzantine empire, and in Islamic territories – unsophisticated. The contrast became plain when the Crusades sent the feudal hosts into the eastern lands. It was the Frankish knights who were progressively civilized by association with superior cultures; it was they who came to assimilate to the life-styles, and eventually to the learning, of the east. Some of it even filtered back to the west through their agency. Byzantium had itself retained residual links with the west: there was an exarch in Ravenna until the final end of the Roman world, and Venice, whose contacts with Constantinople were mostly commercial, showed plainly Byzantine influence in its architectural splendour. This perspective needs to be kept in mind, for to modern judgement medieval Christianity has sometimes been envisaged in highly idealized sequences – a notion engendered by the musings of A.W.N. Pugin, John Ruskin and William Morris, by the penchant for the Gothic style in buildings and in taste, and by a whole field full of earthy characters who are supposed to have typified the rude exuberance and vitality of a people still rooted in natural and deliciously vulgar manners – before the Puritans got their hands on them. Chaucer has got a lot to answer for. But compared with the Byzantine and Islamic east (and south) Catholic Europe was poor in wealth, underdone in culture, and only rather clumsily engaged with the problems annexed to reconciling feudal monarchy with the concepts of universal order inherited from the collapsed Roman world. Yet the papacy had retained some grasp upon the idea of universal sovereignty: hence at least part of the clash of papal claims with feudal practice. Hobbes was correct in his famous observation that the papacy was 'the ghost of the deceased Roman Empire sitting crowned upon the grave thereof.'

For the papacy, Christendom represented the old Ciceronian concept of commonwealth. Its vision of the emperor – whose powers were divine, and were not subject to any other authority – was met in the succession of St Peter. This was the idea of the papacy, expressed in different language, promoted by Gregory VII, who reigned from St Peter's chair after 1073, and who fashioned the ideological armoury that engaged medieval feudal monarchy. The Frankish and Germanic kings, despite their enormous respect for the memory of the fading imperial order, saw sovereignty in their precedence over the feudal host; they were the hereditary descendants of those first raised on the shields of their victorious warriors, whose kingdom incorporated a hierarchy of obligations and loyalties. This was all considerably removed from Augustine's concept of the Christian state that encompassed the entire world, and which depended on moral and spiritual ties – not blood ones – without which government became nothing but 'highway robbery on a large scale'. When *sacerdotium* and *imperium* came into disagreement, as they did in the evolution of medieval Christendom, the incompatibilities of the two ideas of sovereignty, of the papacy and of the kings, were exhibited in a very primal manner.

Most of the claims to authority over temporal rulers promoted by the papacy have since lapsed. The force of historical circumstance, in the rise of the modern nation state, has meant that there is no longer a single world order to which Christian government could correspond or could embody, let alone the religious uniformity that is necessary for its practical operation. None of the papal claims to temporal jurisdiction were advanced as infallible teaching, providentially, and when the last remnants of the pope's own territories were seized by the Italian liberals in the *Risorgimento* of the nineteenth century, the whole concept of mixing spiritual and temporal jurisdiction finally disintegrated. Momentous as the conflicts attendant upon the advance of papal claims were in the medieval world, however, they should not be allowed to obscure the advances of the Catholic Church which occurred steadily in these centuries.

With the reconquest of Spain from the Moors throughout the Middle Ages, and ending in 1492, and the creation of the kingdom of Prussia in the thirteenth century by eastern expansion, western Europe achieved a reasonably uniform Catholic presence. Everywhere the provinces and dioceses of the Church consolidated advance and were regularized by the growth of centralism and bureaucracy in Rome. The Church was not static. There were

A 14th-century representation of Islamic warriors laying siege to a fortress. Such a scene, with the weaponry appropriate to an earlier era, must have been witnessed when Arab forces overran the Holy Land provinces of the Byzantine Empire in the 7th century.

reform impulses which periodically visited even the remotest corners of western Christendom; there were changes in the style and influence of the monastic orders; there was the appearance of universities and schools and numerous Christian guilds and fraternities; and there was external expansion, promoted within the Crusading ideal.

There was, on the other hand, also a uniform survival of superstition and pagan practice, especially in the country areas (which meant most areas, since the populations were overwhelmingly rural). Some of these observances and rites were absorbed by the Church and given a Christian gloss; many others simply co-existed with the Faith and reappeared on the surface of official life from time to time. There was also heresy: a feature perhaps inadequately evaluated by the modern mind, no longer able to comprehend how medieval authorities, both lay and clerical, could have allowed themselves to take such extreme measures in order to extirpate unorthodox opinion. Modern people no longer think, as medieval Christians did, in terms of organic unities. The Church was envisaged as the seamless robe of Christ; its very ecclesiology required uniformity of belief to guarantee its authority. Truth was determined by what was received as truth everywhere – the Church was *Catholic*. Belief was not a matter of sound judgement made by individuals in relation to intellectual propositions or emotional appeal – as it might be for people today – but of *allegiance* to a divine institution which was, as it was thought, the very body of Christ in the world. Religious truth was about eternal salvation.

If medieval Catholicism looks authoritarian to modern observers it is because it undoubtedly was; medieval Christians were as insistent on correct attitudes to the Faith as people now are towards, for example, race or sexual equality. The difference is that medieval people operated within a society that assumed an organic unity and we do not. The modern world admires medieval craftsmanship and art, yet is repelled by its understanding of religion. This becomes most evident when modern commentators seek to interpret that most characteristic ideal of medieval religion, the Crusade.

In more recent attitudes to the Crusades, it is cultural and religious insensitivity towards the invaded Islamic people that seems to have elicited disquiet within western liberal opinion. There are periodic demands – not resisted by the Churches – that apologies should be made by Christian bodies for the Crusades. Perhaps, however, a balance of remorse might be achieved if the Islamic bodies were, in turn, asked to apologize for their own invasions of the Byzantine provinces and the Holy Land some three-and-a-half centuries before. Then peaceful Christian populations were overrun amid scenes of very considerable violence, which had never been forgotten and which helped to inspire the Crusading ideal. Wisdom, however, would

The loss of the Byzantine Holy Land was never forgotten, and atrocities committed there in the second half of the 10th century prompted Pope Urban II to appeal to the conscience of Europe to seek military action for their recovery. He called for a crusade at the Council of Clermont in 1095.

suggest allowing the past its own integrity; the point is that the Crusades today are evaluated in a context, and with a passion, which has departed from academic detachment.

Why did Pope Urban II preach a crusade at the Council of Clermont in 1095? The effect was the imperfect, and ultimately unsuccessful, export of feudal monarchy to the Holy Land and to parts of Anatolia; employment for the surplus nobility of western Europe; a seizure of land; a further souring of relationships between eastern and western Christianity. But the greater result, and the purpose for which Urban II initiated the whole enterprise, was the pursuit of an ideal: access to the holy places. To understand the

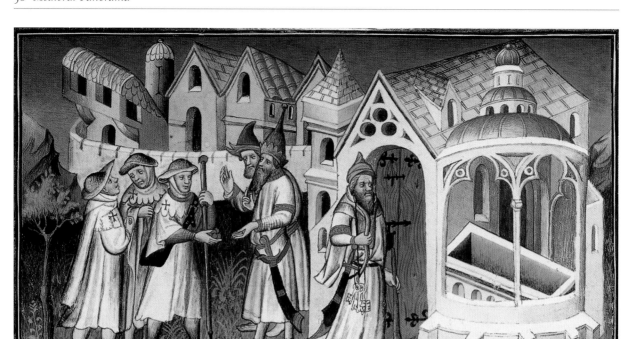

ABOVE Christian pilgrims with staff, and cross badge, seek admission to the Church of the Holy Sepulchre in Jerusalem. Moslem guards are shown with arms and keys. The tomb itself, and the dome raised above it, are highly stylized representations. The illustration is from a 14th-century manuscript of Riccoldo da Monte di Croce's account of his travels.

RIGHT The relics of saints were carried far, and those believed to be of St James the Apostle reached Galicia in Spain. The city of Compostela rose as a great pilgrim centre in consequence, and here may be seen the silver reliquary containing his bones.

importance of the Crusades it is necessary to appreciate how deeply medieval Catholicism was committed to pilgrimage. To go on a pilgrimage was a solemn and serious undertaking: yet most knowledge of pilgrimage today derives from Chaucer's amusing and crude caricature. In the surviving solemnity of pilgrimage in modern Islam one may still see something of the original purpose. In medieval Christendom there were hallowed and celebrated pilgrim routes, with many local sanctuaries *en route*, to which men and women resorted in the belief that some actual contact with the remains of the blessed would secure spiritual benefit.

The pilgrims often travelled enormous distances – to the holy city of Rome, sanctified by the bones of St Peter and St Paul, to the tomb of St James at Compostela in Galicia, to the body of St Mark in Venice (stolen from Alexandria, a classic *coup*, so the Venetians imagined, for Venetian enterprise), to the shrine of St Thomas of Canterbury. And they also went to Jerusalem. They went there before the Crusades, when a small Christian presence still tended the holy places. To secure the tomb of Christ, the very

The Crusaders enter Jerusalem in July 1099. The Latin Kingdom that they set up included a Catholic Patriarch and the restoration of the Christian shrines. Many of the traditional holy places, in sites venerated since the time of Christ himself, remained in Byzantine Orthodox hands, and as a consequence the Crusaders sometimes identified new sites under their own control. Hence the paradox, which troubles modern visitors, that shrines in the Holy Land occasionally exist in apparently rival locations.

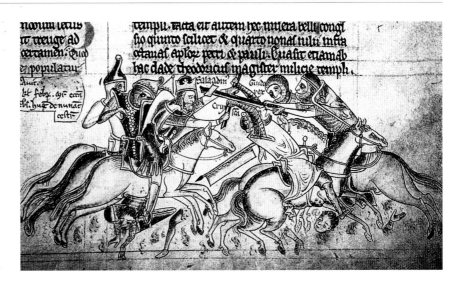

LEFT The main entrance to the Church of the Holy Sepulchre in Jerusalem, rebuilt by the Crusaders. The *edicule* of the *Anástasis* – the canopy over the remnants of the tomb of Christ, and therefore the scene of the Resurrection – is to the left inside the door.

RIGHT The Battle of Hattin in 1187 was a decisive moment in the collapse of the Latin Kingdoms in the Holy Land. By this time the dress and weaponry of Christian and Moslem fighters were very similar: mutual cultural assimilation was a characteristic of the two centuries of the western presence in the Holy Land.

BELOW The Frankish Knights sacked Constantinople in the Fourth Crusade, 1204: many treasures ended up at St Mark's in Venice, for it was the Venetians who had provided transport for the Crusade. This enamel panel, which is among them, dates from around 1130, and depicts the Resurrection. Christians in the Orthodox tradition have never forgotten the appalling desecration of the city's churches. The papacy condemned it at the time.

scene of the Resurrection, was an aspiration which had remained in the Christian mind ever since the Islamic conquests. The Caliph al-Hakim's destruction of the tomb (leaving only the base) in 1009, and the simultaneous razing of many Christian basilicas and churches in the Holy Land, provided ample evidence that the most sacred sites of the Christian world were under threat. The Crusaders, when they reached Jerusalem, were to enclose what remained of the tomb of Christ with a rebuilt domed Church: it was what the Crusades were all about.

In 1071, the Byzantine empire lost its remaining Middle Eastern provinces to Islam at the Battle of Manzikert, and it was by then already clear that any attempt to recover the Holy Land itself would have to come from the Catholic west and not from the progressively enfeebled Byzantine state. The Crusades established Latin kingdoms in which the feudal lords, granted lands and titles as a reward for their service to the cause of religion, reproduced the social arrangements of western Europe. They lasted, however, only until 1291 and the fall of Acre to Islamic forces. Jerusalem itself returned to Islamic rule following Saladin's success at Hattin in 1187. There were several Crusades, and in the centuries following the evacuation of the Latin kingdoms popes occasionally returned to the idea, but in vain. The Fourth Crusade, in 1204, was diverted by the Venetians, the carriers, into an assault, only too successful, on Constantinople. To the horror of the Christian world, east and west, the greatest city in Christendom was ransacked and despoiled, its relics and treasures removed to western churches and to the chapels of the nobility. Nothing so terribly illustrated the gulf that had opened up between Catholic and Orthodox Christianity. The Pope condemned the sack of Constantinople.

The popes were also careful, during the Crusades, to make it plain that there should be no forceful conversion of Moslems: Innocent IV spelled this out in detail, though he, and other preachers of Crusade, also clearly maintained that force to allow the recovery of the Holy Land itself was legitimate. It was the Crusades that assisted the definition of what constituted a 'Just War': proportionality, the viability of successful attainment of desired objectives, respect for non-combatants, and so forth. The so-called Just War 'theory', for which there has been a modern Christian vogue, was not in reality a theory at all, however. It represented a code of conduct appropriate in the highly localized and largely dynastic skirmishes of feudal society in the western European countries where the notion of a Just War took its origins. It was never effectively observed even in them, never acquired general assent, and is certainly quite inoperable in the confrontation of the nation-states of the modern world with their collectivist resources and efficient weaponry. In the Crusades, however, Just War conditions often could be met, as the civilized exchanges, which occurred between Islamic and Christian commanders, indicated. Many of the truces that were arranged were violated, however; many words of honour pledged were in the event dishonoured. But there were attempts at an ideal here, and the Crusader states, once established, showed how courtesies and chivalrous conduct in warfare could sometimes extend beyond purely military considerations. The feudal knights rapidly succumbed to the allure of eastern lifestyles, and in manners and dress the Frankish knights ended up looking and behaving rather like the Islamic rulers they had displaced.

The orders of Military Knights were an important development of the Crusades, and were a major influence in the way Catholicism defined its mission. The orders consisted of noblemen who took monastic vows, and whose functions were increasingly military after the Crusades began. Though they were always real knights, fighting men, their vows and manner of living really was monastic: reforms were made to secure purity of purpose under the guidance of St Bernard of Clairvaux, who had himself preached a crusade in 1146. To the medieval mind there was no incompatibility between the simultaneous profession of military and monastic vocations. The Knights of St John of Jerusalem, the Hospitallers, probably began around 1070; the Templars were more certainly founded in 1120; the Teutonic Knights were established in 1191 with the support of the merchants of Lübeck. The Spanish Crusades, the *Reconquista*, had the orders of Calatrava, Alcántara and Santiago.

In the provision of what would today be called social services, as well as in guardianship of the pilgrim routes, the Military Knights were enlightened and inventive. The Hospitallers, for example, employed nursing sisters in their enormous Jerusalem hospital a thousand years before Florence Nightingale.

OPPOSITE St Bernard of Clairvaux preaching the Second Crusade before King Louis VII of France at Vézelay in 1146. Bernard, who was the greatest monastic reformer of his day, was also spiritual adviser to the Knights Templar. A page from the 15th-century *Les Passages d'Outre Mer* by Sebastien Mamerot de Soissons.

que la terre sainte z les xpri
ens vpristiens y demourans
feussent secourus et guidés
contre ses impitueulx assaulx
et leurs trefaulceurs et autres
ennemis. et ouurant le tresor
de leglise donna plain pardon
et remission de paine z de
coulpe de tous uices atoue
et a ving chascun de ceulx q

en faueur et pour aidier la ter
re sainte prendroient lenseigne
de la sainte Croix z yroient
en cestui voyage. Et combien
quil y eust lors es diuerses
parties de vpristiente plusieurs
seigneurs duieux z prelatz
Toutesfois seiuisoit pour
celui temps icelluy comme
lestoit le iournal au vint du

INFIRMIS·SERVIRE
FIRMISSIMVM REGNARE.

The Knights Hospitaller, or the Order of St John of Jerusalem, was established just prior to the Crusades to provide medical care for those on pilgrimage to the Holy Land. This 16th-century engraving, by Philippe Thomassin, shows part of their famous hospital in Jerusalem.

Ancient Greek knowledge of medicine, learned from Islamic doctors, was also used by the Hospitallers, and transmitted back to Europe. In addition, the Knights developed banking services, with Arab specialists conducting transactions for them in the money markets of Cairo and Baghdad, so avoiding problems raised by the Christian prohibition of usury. Bills of exchange were developed by the Orders. Pilgrims began to be transported from Europe in the Orders' own ships; thus travel in the cross-Mediterranean sea-routes was systematized independently of the dictates of trade, although the Orders themselves were not backward in exploiting trading opportunities.

ABOVE LEFT After the evacuation of the Holy Land, which took place in stages dictated by Islamic advance, the Knights Hospitaller sought refuge first in Cyprus and then in the island of Rhodes – where they built a citadel. They were harried by Islamic forces, however, and eventually, in 1522, after a prolonged siege, they were allowed to leave with honour and eventually settled in Malta. A 15th-century illustration of the siege.

ABOVE RIGHT The Teutonic Knights, originally founded by merchants of Lübeck, concentrated on the advance of Christianity in northern Europe after the fall of the Holy Land. It was they who organized the systematic settlement of the pagan lands that then became Prussia.

The growing wealth and prestige of the Military Orders in European countries made their influence in the Church and in society significant, and occasionally attracted the avarice of nobles and kings. It was inside Europe that the Teutonic Knights performed their greatest service for Christendom. They conquered the pagan lands between the Catholic west and the Russian Orthodox east in the fourteenth century, and the resulting planned German settlement was the foundation of what in the thirteenth century became the kingdom of Prussia. The Knights' silver and black cross is to this day the military insignia of the German armed forces.

The wealth of the Templars, and especially of the Paris Temple, which was the centre of the European money market, was attacked by the French monarchy early in the fourteenth century. The Templars were always regarded as being secretive, and this encouraged the accumulation of fantastic rumours about the nature of the Order and the ready supposition of scandalous irregularities. The matter is especially of note because there are modern resonances. Accusations began of blasphemous secret rites, heretical beliefs and sexual perversions. Many of these came from areas in the south-west of France, which had been the heartlands of the Albigensian heresy, suppressed some twenty years before. The Albigensians had espoused ascetic ideals that contrasted with what was alleged of Templar practices; these added popular appeal to the case against the Order. A vacillating papacy and a strong French monarch, Philip IV, opened the way for the suppression of the Templars; after 1307 over fifteen thousand were arrested and many were executed, property was confiscated throughout Europe. Now the supposed secrets of the Templars, most of which were palpable falsehoods extracted from revived Albigensian fantasies, have in our own day formed the basis of popular accounts of hidden codes, which are claimed to indicate conspiracies by the Catholic Church to cover up what are represented as discreditable episodes in the origin of Christianity itself.

The Crusade in Spain was the longest and, in the expulsion of Islam from territories formerly Christian, the most successful. The Islamic invasions had begun in 712, and the final defeat of the Moors at Granada was in 1492. Warfare was intermittent during all these centuries, with some districts changing hands quite frequently. In fact, except for a clearly recognizable heartland, the Islamic presence was never very stable, and never homogeneous. Towns were patchworks of Arab and Christian quarters, with a Berber underclass, and the countryside was in many places largely Christian. In Spain, the Christian Church had always exhibited distinctive local features, bearing strong traces of the original Visigothic kingdoms – which had converted to the faith shortly after their establishment, sometimes in an Arian version. Catholicism became recognized by the time the Moorish presence had consolidated itself; the Church in Spain before the conquests was internationally renowned for its strength and splendour. In scholars such as St Isidore of Seville, who died in 636, it had achieved a golden age. Its Visigothic style of worship, the Mozarabic rite, although overlaid by the Roman rite brought to Spain by the Cluniac monks in the eleventh century, has continued in some churches in revived forms to the present day. The relationship of Moors and Christians was often close: Moors unable to drink alcohol publicly because of Islamic prohibition were to be found taking wine in Christian taverns.

The Reconquest had about it the characteristics of a civil war. The truth is that 'Moorish society' was internally divided. The number of Arabs was relatively small, and constituted an upper class; most of those who came to Spain were Berber tribesmen who were regarded by the Arabs as social inferiors but who were needed as fighters. Islam itself was periodically divided by revivalist movements, spread from North Africa. Their ascetic and puritan exponents were disdainful of the soft life in which the Spanish Moslems appeared to luxuriate: a situation comparable to the accusations made against the Frankish knights who settled in the Holy Land. There was a long history of literary vituperation of the Moors in Spain until late in the nineteenth century, when unexpectedly the Moors came into fashion.

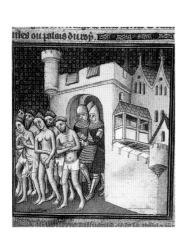

The Albigensians or Cathars were 13th-century heretics whose heartlands were in the south-west of France. They taught an extreme puritanism, rejected any but the 'elect', denied ecclesiastical authority, and evolved strange interpretations of biblical texts. In 1209, the entire city of Carcassonne was emptied of its population in an attempt to extirpate the extremists.

Today, a markedly uncritical attitude to Moorish Spain seems prevalent. It derives, however, almost wholly from artistic and cultural judgement. The political and social arrangements of the Moors are generally ignored by the modern enthusiasts, for Moorish Spain comprised a series of autocracies which completely failed to develop anything like the representative institutions, the judicial system, or the concepts of individual liberty that evolved in medieval Europe. It was, additionally, a slave society, with a slave economy. All those placid courtyards and sparkling fountains, that poetry and art, rested upon the existence of one of the largest slave populations the world has ever seen. In the absence of any doctrine of individual rights, the slaves of the Moors were also subject to infelicitous indignities: at the court of Cordova in the tenth century, at the very height of that great city's most astonishing artistic accomplishments, the Emir maintained a palace harem of 6,000 women and 13,000 young boys. It is not surprising that Spanish Christians found Moorish moral standards defective, nor that they should have sought what is now termed regime change.

The suppression of the Knights Templar – at the time the major west European bankers – by King Philip IV of France, at the start of the 14th century, was accompanied by a profusion of hostile propaganda. The Knights were accused of grave moral offences and numerous financial improprieties. Some of the charges relating to their supposed unorthodox religious convictions are still evidently capable of attracting belief today.

Yet the relations of Moors and Christians allowed the transmission of scholarship and learning to medieval Europe. The libraries of Christian Spain yielded up early Christian writings; Greek medical and philosophical thought came through texts translated from Arabic to Latin. The slave state of Cordova may have sustained sexual customs that the Christians found anathema, but the city also produced Averroës in the mid-twelfth century – a scholar of Greek thought to whose learning there are over five hundred references in the works of St Thomas Aquinas. Moorish Islam, for its part, drew much inspiration from Christian culture; it was not, however, the culture of the feudal, Catholic west, but of the Byzantine east.

The real contrast is not between Moorish Spain and Catholic Europe, but between Moorish Spain and Byzantium. For Constantinople offered an example in art and culture as important as Baghdad. It is always necessary to remember, in any assessment of medieval Catholicism, that it was Byzantium which was, to non-European observers, the visible embodiment of Christian society. When the Ottoman Turks eventually overran Constantinople they did so as the barbarians had invaded the Roman empire – not to destroy it, but to be enriched by it. Thus when, in 936, the Emir of

Cordova, Abd al-Rahman III, began to build himself a new palace (the Madinat al-Zahra) it was a Christian bishop, Recemund of Elvira, who was employed to decorate it in the Byzantine style, and craftsmen were imported from Constantinople. The Byzantine emperor himself, Porphyrogenitus, supplied 140 marble columns.

The Reconquest in Spain was accompanied by every species of propagandist mutual recrimination, and a parade of differences. And the differences were very great. Yet at many levels Catholicism and Islam co-existed reasonably well. Lists of bishops show that many bore Islamic names, evidence of their cultural assimilation; the dress of Moors and Christians was identical. The feudal kingdoms which were set up as the Christian Reconquest advanced were more foreign to the indigenous Christian populations than the decadent remnants of the departing Moorish courts.

Two footnotes can be added. The first concerns the development of the notorious Spanish Inquisition. During the eleventh and twelfth centuries Sufist brotherhoods introduced puritanical reformation to Moorish Islam, in a revolution of attitudes comparable to, if more radical than, the European reforms of the Catholic religious orders. Late in the twelfth century this led to the institution of Islamic courts to punish heresy – and also to the introduction of extremely severe methods of torture, used to extract confessions. When the first Catholic Inquisition was set up in Castile, in 1478, it employed, in addition to Roman procedures, well established in some European countries, practices already familiar and up and running used in the existing heresy courts of Islamic Spain. There is a sense in which the notorious Spanish Inquisition was a Moorish legacy.

The second footnote is about the extension of the Spanish Crusade overseas. In many ways the Spanish and Portuguese conquests in the New World, towards the close of the Middle Ages, were a continuation of the old Crusading ideal: for claiming new lands for the Cross, for bringing Christian understanding to peoples who practised human blood sacrifice. Just as the Crusades in the Holy Land adhered to worldly ambitions and the allure of wealth and title as well as to religion, so the expeditions to the Americas and to the east were also associated with material interests. There was always, however, a robust religious motivation: the vision of a revived Christendom, enlarged and Catholic. There was a direct continuity, from the expulsion of the Moors in Spain to the missions in America. Juan Ponce de León, soldier and adventurer, had been Commander at the fall of Granada in 1492. Later he sailed across the Atlantic and in 1513 up the coast of a still unknown land of lush greenness and many flowers: after these last the Spaniards called it Florida. The body of Ponce de León, last of the Crusaders, first of the Conquistadors, may still be visited at his marble tomb in the cathedral of St Juan de Puerto Rico.

OPPOSITE The expulsion of the Moors from Spain took place over many centuries and came at the end to have something of the characteristics of a series of civil wars. In this fifteenth-century Spanish depiction of the Battle of Puig, in 1237, St James of Compostela (with halo) comes to the aid of King James I's Aragonese army. The *Reconquista* was completed with the fall of Granada in 1492.

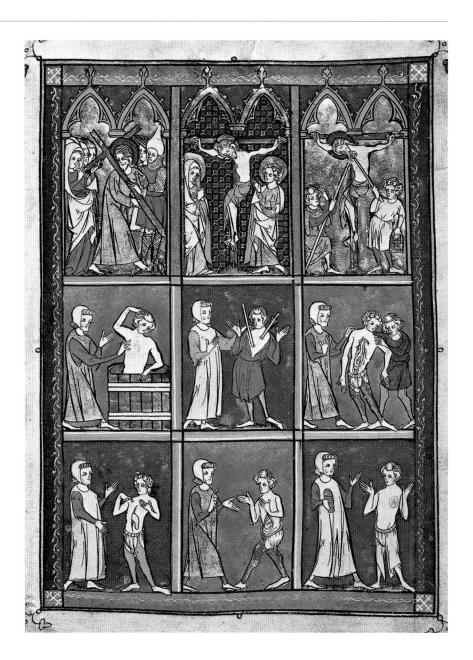

Arab learning developed ancient Greek knowledge of medicine, and the great Arab medical schools transmitted it to Europe in the Middle Ages. This illustration from a 13th-century translation of Roger of Salerno's *Chirugia* depicts various treatments for wounds.

Spain was not the only place from which Catholic Europe derived new knowledge of the learning of Antiquity. The Crusades took relatively unsophisticated western Europeans to the centres of Byzantine scholarship and to libraries and schools where Arab translations of the Greek texts were available – in Sicily, and Anatolia in particular. The result was the 'Twelfth Century Renaissance', the rediscovery of the works of Aristotle and other Greek writers; it was seen in the recovery of Roman thought through the study of Roman Law, and the foundation of the great Law Schools. Early Jewish texts came from Alexandria as well as Spain. The congruence of these sources, and the surviving monastic learning of the west, produced medieval Scholasticism. The reception of the ideas of the Greek Sophists acquainted Catholic scholars with a world of social values quite separable from religious sanction. Political society no longer seemed dependent upon divine dispensation, or Gelasian Swords, or the different claims of popes and emperors, but upon its own reasoned purposes. The state existed to secure the ends of good citizenship, and needed no external authority. The view of government being revived, of course, reflected the vanished conditions of the Greek *polis*, and required adjustment before it could be entertained as the measure of feudal monarchy. Existing Catholic scholarship came down from the Fathers of the Church – who had themselves been indebted to classical learning.

The scene of convergence was the university or, more explicitly, the Universities of Padua, Paris and Oxford, the leading institutions dominated by the new Mendicant orders, in which there was, for the first time, a lay element. The Church authorities correctly recognized some essential incompatibilities between Aristotelian speculation and received understanding of the basis of intellectual authority. The new learning was accordingly banned at the University of Paris in 1210. There was never conscientious observance of the prohibition, however, and the Church, instead, reversed into a fulsome embrace of the Aristotelian *Aufklärung*.

The rise of the European universities in the 12th and 13th centuries responded to the new learning – of which Scholastic Philosophy was a part. They allowed a freedom for the discussion of ideas unknown since Antiquity. Amalric of Bena is here shown addressing his students at the University of Paris, the greatest of the new centres of learning.

Q celi temps flourssoit a paris philosophie et toute clergie. et ŷestoit lestude si grant et en si grant auctorite: que len ne trueuc pas que

monde. Si nestoit pas tant seulemēt pour le delitable lieu ne pour la pleute des biens qui en la cite labundeut: mes pour la pais et pour la franchise que li bons rois looŷs auoit touz iours portee. et que li rois phelippes ses fuz

The Dominican friar Albertus Magnus, and his pupil Thomas Aquinas (another Dominican) led the assimilation of intellectual disciplines. Aquinas became the most respected of all Catholic philosophers, and his great *Summa Theologica* the most well-known (though certainly not the most widely read) work of Catholic systematic philosophy. By the time of his death, in 1274, he had established a new intellectual orthodoxy. Harmony and synthesis: his conflation of Aristotelian reason and categorizing with Catholic revelation and dogmatics is completely incorporative; it reads like one of those modern Ph.D. theses in which all the evidence is bent and related to illuminate and expose a particular theme – or, as they say, a theory of everything. Aquinas did not intend to depart from the general conclusions of accepted Christian thought, and did not do so, either in the overall construction of theology or in the themes of human association. He sought, instead, to explain what they mean in relation to Christian ideas of Revelation as a whole. For this he expounded a hierarchy of laws, Eternal and Natural, Divine and Human. When applied to the issues of the times, and especially to the conflict between the jurisdictions of *sacerdotium* and *imperium*, his system appears moderate: while confessing the Church's spiritual authority to be superior, he declined to follow the inclination of the canon lawyers to express it as legal supremacy.

The revival of Aristotle which came from Averroist sources – from Spain – in the thirteenth century, however, was less restrained, and contained within itself philosophical views about the nature of human society which always had the potential to escape from traditional Catholic teaching. Marsiglio of Padua's *Defensor Pacis*, produced in 1324, was a decisive rejection of papal claims to *plenitudo potestatis*, to supreme authority, based upon acceptance of Aristotelian attitudes to the natural origins of civil authority. For Marsiglio, spiritual authority had only theoretical rights over governments; the state had a moral authority of its own which did not need divine sanction. He also outlined an actual scheme for the government of the Church by an institutionalized and representative general council.

William of Occam, the fourteenth-century Franciscan, also wrote in favour of a broadly based general council to govern the Church, and so to curb the absolutism of the papacy. His writings gave a less comprehensive account of the nature of authority than Marsiglio's, but also depended on Averroist interpretations of Aristotle's thought. His writings tended, also, to undermine papalist claims to superiority over civil rulers. Ultimately a rather conservative analyst, he nevertheless sought to return to the Gelasian distinction of spiritual and temporal powers, existing in a permanent state of mutual dependence and balance.

Clement V became Pope in 1305; he was Archbishop of Bordeaux. The removal of the papacy to Avignon (which became a papal enclave in France

OPPOSITE St Thomas Aquinas, a portrait attributed to Botticelli, *c*.1481. The most influential of the Scholastic philosophers (the 'Angelic Doctor'), and a Dominican friar – an order that came to be noted for its educational and intellectual enterprise. To this day, his interpretation of universal knowledge is included in the curriculae of Catholic seminaries.

after 1348) for seventy-five years, after Clement V's departure from Rome in 1309, and followed, from 1378 to 1415, by the 'Great Schism', when there were at one time three popes, gave a kind of evidential basis to theoretical and reasoned critiques of papal claims to authority. The popes at Avignon, though persisting in formal (and sometimes asserted) independence, came generally under the influence of the French monarchy. These were not years of *stasis*, however. It was at Avignon that the papacy, and the canon lawyers, began to accumulate bureaucratic institutions, leading to an enhanced

Papal residence at Avignon for three-quarters of a century, after 1309, brought the central institutions of the Church under the influence of the French monarchy. In fact, these were years of very fruitful advance in ecclesiastical bureaucracy, but there was still almost universal relief when the curia returned to Rome – the scene shown here by Vasari.

centralization – and papalization – of the Church. The number of appeals to the papacy for the settlement of administrative and disputed issues, from all over the Catholic world, also increased. By the time of the Council of Constance in 1415, which ended the schism, the machinery of papal government had expanded in response to this volume of business. The 'Conciliar Theory' of ecclesiology, indeed, may in some sense be recognized as a reaction not only to papal claims to *plenitudo potestatis* but as a symptom of unease about the degree of centralization felt by the archbishops of the Catholic provinces. It was also a call for internal reform of clerical abuses.

There had, in fact, been a fairly consistent tradition of Church reforms throughout the Middle Ages – receiving its most vibrant impulses at the Lateran Council summoned by Innocent III in 1215. The council had addressed the issues of secular interference with episcopal appointments, priestly duties, the punishment of heretics, and so forth. In these ways it was a continuation of the pattern of clerical reform established by Gregory VII (Hildebrand). That was towards the end of the eleventh century. Gregory VII also issued *Dictatus Papae* in 1075, a major statement of papal claims to temporal as well as spiritual authority – not a claim to direct government, except within the States of the Church, but to the scrutiny of the conduct of secular rulers, and with the rights of excommunication, deposition, and the release of subjects from the obligation of obedience. Thus was established, in a notably precise form, the papal case that eventually resulted in the famous 'Investiture Controversy' of papacy and the civil powers.

The immediate matter of contention was papal denial of the right of secular rulers to invest bishops in their office, a custom inseparable from the existence, throughout most of western Europe, of proprietary churches built and maintained by princes, nobles and landowners. Later disputes extended to the right of the popes to confirm Imperial elections: this was finally

ABOVE Pope Innocent III. A 13th-century fresco from the Monastery of San Benedetto, Subiaco.

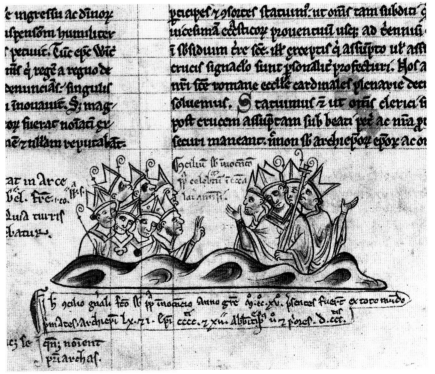

RIGHT Innocent III summoned the Lateran Council in 1215, in an attempt to revivify reforming ideas. Accretions of bad practice were not solely due to clerical sloth or indiscipline but often derived from lay, and especially royal, incursions into ecclesiastical administration. This drawing of the assembled bishops comes from Matthew Paris's *Chronica majora*, of the 13th century.

denied by the Declaration of Rense in 1338, promulgated by the Imperial Electors themselves. The assertion of very extensive papal jurisdiction over temporal governance, made most unambiguously in Boniface VIII's bull *Unam Sanctam* in 1302, was not, therefore, successful in producing real effect. The claims were never withdrawn; the imperial parties never sought to test them very radically. The whole matter, however, elicited an informed and often very scholarly body of polemical writing across Europe, precipitated the Avignon papacy, and, in the growth of conciliar theory, established a critique of papal ecclesiology which, after the Council of Basle in 1432, lay dormant until the Reformation. At Basle, the assembled bishops called upon the pope to be subordinate to the decisions of General Councils. To summarise late medieval Catholicism around these controversies, as is so often

The bull *Unam Sanctam*, issued in 1302, was the furthest extension of papal authority over temporal power ever made, but had very limited effect. Here, Boniface III, author of the bull, presides over a consistory of cardinals; from the 14th-century *Decretals of Boniface VIII* in the British Library.

done, however, is to miss the reforming impulses operating within the leadership of the Church during these centuries.

It was a time of extraordinary religious vitality. This may be seen, paradoxically, in the reappearance of heresy on a significant scale. Unorthodox opinions about the nature of the faith are not always generated by public disgust at clerical abuses or the resurgence of superstition: they often indicate a yearning for pristine values, and are a sign of vitality. Apathy can kill, whereas error can stimulate. Thus the Albigensians (Cathars) and the Waldensians, at the end of the twelfth century, and the Lollards and the Hussites in the fifteenth, may in some senses be judged an indication that for the reformer the pursuit of the supposed original purity of early Christianity should be the essential agenda of a living Church. In many places these were popular movements; there was also a strong lay element.

St Francis of Assisi, by Giovanni
Bellini, 1480. The Saint himself,
and his followers, sought poverty
through the renunciation of worldly
possessions in order to be of
service to the Church and its
mission. His sense of the unity of
the creation was symbolized in his
communion with animals, and the
intensity of his devotional life was
rewarded with the *stigmata* upon
his hands. Here he is represented
in a wilderness landscape, his arms
extended in prayer.

They had different emphases: the Albigensians were ascetic and sought
purity, the later heretics were Biblicist and looked to a more accessible structure of Church government.

In the mainstream Church, meanwhile, real reform was all along proceeding. At its heart was monastic revival. The initial intention was similar to that
of the heretics in at least one important particular: a desire to return the
monastic ideal to the discipline and spiritual immediacy of the Desert
Fathers. In the eleventh century, Nilus of Calabria settled a monastic community in the Alban Hills of Rome, based on the rule of St Basil and using the
Greek rite. Others attempted a return to early Benedictine practice, less
encumbered by material preoccupations and austere in devotional styles. The
result was the Carthusians, founded in 1084, the Cistercians in 1098, and
the Augustinians, founded sometime in the middle of the eleventh century.

The Mendicant orders set up early in the thirteenth century – the Franciscans and the Dominicans – also aspired to simplicity. The Franciscans were noted for popular preaching, addressing their message in the urban centres which at the time were developing through the guilds and the entrepreneurial skills of a growing class of men free from the thrall of rural feudal deference. St Francis himself, who died in 1226, was inspired by a personal need to divest himself of the priorities of the world and to follow Christ in literal poverty and simplicity. The Dominicans were also popular preachers, and many were scholars of distinction. St Dominic, who died in 1221, was concerned with the intellectual defeat of heresy. The friars have remained essential components of Catholic Christianity ever since, and it would be difficult to understand the significance of Scholastic philosophy

An itinerant friar preaching to the people. It was usual – as here – for friars to give their exhortations at church doors, common places for meetings and announcements.

for Christian learning without an appreciation of their contribution. As popular preachers the friars sometimes acquired truly international renown – the Dominican St Vincent Ferrer, for example, spent the first half of his life teaching in the University of Valencia, yet was beloved of the simple people as he travelled through Europe for the rest of his life, speaking to them of the mysteries of the Faith. He was canonized in 1455, forty years after his death,

The work of St Dominic (left) is symbolized by the dogs who are rescuing sheep from wolves. St Peter Martyr (right) is disputing with heretics and unbelievers. A fresco of 1355 by Andrea da Firenze in Santa Maria Novella in Florence.

and is always represented iconographically with the wings of an angel, a memory of the resonance of his heavenly words. It was the friars who travelled with the merchants and explorers to the lands overseas. In the fourteenth century there were friars in China, preaching to the subjects of the Mongol emperors. Early in the sixteenth century they were leading missions to the Indians of the New World.

PAVLVS·III·PONTIFEX·MAXIMVS
CONSTITVENDAE·CHRISTIANAE
DISCIPLINAE·CAVSA
TRIDENTI·CONCILIVM·CELEBRAT
ANNO·SALVTIS·CIƆIƆXLVI

4
Reformation

The medieval reform tradition in the Catholic Church had not resulted in a consistent programme, nor had it met, except in a very short-term perspective, the various agendas pressing for action. In each age and in each place the satisfaction of one set of grievances or ideals does little to pre-empt the emergence of new ones: it is the way of all things. Change in the medieval world was necessarily uneven; there were always some, often in the highest centres of authority, who were left behind in the progress of opinion, and with whom historical memory has dealt unkindly, and there were always some others who differed about the application of the changes that had been agreed. The Church in the world is conducted by men and not by angels. Some changes were widely recognized as desirable and yet little of any practical effect resulted – in 1311 the Council of Vienne considered reforms at length, and especially dwelt upon issues related to clerical morals, indulgences, and the pervasiveness of poor clerical education; yet few reforms were put in place as a result. It is also true that the context in which the concept of reform presented itself was forever being transformed; the very conditions were unstable, and that, reasonably enough, elicited caution in those who were entrusted with the maintenance and advance of an institution that judged itself, and thought, in terms of centuries.

The sixteenth-century Church therefore inherited a preparedness for change but no sustained reform agenda. Existing pressures for an open Bible – for a vernacular text – for the abolition of clerical abuses, for rationalization of the papal curia, for simplification in the application of canon law in such commonplace matters as matrimonial disputes or testamentary uncertainty, were all received in an atmosphere that seemed capable of response – but which somehow never quite responded on a scale proportionate to the volume of complaint. Yet what surprised men was the actual disruption when it came. The Reformation division seemed out of all proportion to the problems, in view of the history of medieval adaptation and accommodation. Enlightened opinion of the times, the Christian Humanists – the 'New Learning', based on study of Greek texts and Renaissance concepts of human virtue – divided internally. Leading figures in the Church differed about how fundamental the changes they broadly agreed about should be. A schism, which was the eventual outcome, seemed much less likely than a further round of reforms. When the Humanists, the leading intellects of the day, went their different ways over the great issues in public debate there was no certain way of predicting who would remain in the Roman fold and who would depart. Some crossed and re-crossed the lines several times, like Archbishop Cranmer in England. Some of the most celebrated advocates of reform, for example Erasmus of Rotterdam, remained loyal to Rome. What was new about the Reformation of the sixteenth century was not the idea of reforming the Church but radically altered political circumstances.

There had always been abuses in the manner in which the clergy, and the laity, conducted themselves, and there are inevitable shifts in the standards by which institutions judge themselves and are judged: these things take place, however, in a social context, and under political arrangements, which usually operate unevenly. Sometimes there is a dialectical exchange between the Church and the world, the one informing the other about its priorities within an agreed wider frame; sometimes the balance becomes elliptical and a correction occurs which may be so cataclysmic that the frame of reference itself disintegrates. Such an occasion arrived in the Protestant Reformation, and the entire concept of 'Christendom', already flawed by the division of east and west, had either to be modified to allow for the new realities or abandoned altogether.

The Catholic Church contracted in western Europe, as the northern nations repudiated its universal authority. Simultaneously, as it happened, it expanded, and on an enormous scale, through the creation of the Spanish and the Portuguese colonial empires, and through the missionary labours of the new religious orders of the Counter Reformation. The expression 'Counter Reformation' is actually misleading, suggesting, as it does, a reaction to Protestantism. Sixteenth-century reform in the Catholic Church, and the vitality of the religious orders – and especially the measures taken at the Council of Trent after 1545 – were fruits of an ancient root, the Catholic reform tradition. Circumstances required particular changes to meet issues that Protestantism had highlighted, and which had been on reform agendas for over a century. It would be mistaken, however, to assess the adjustments and changes, of which the Council of Trent supplied the programme, as simply a response to the catastrophe that had occurred.

The Reformation, on both sides, was largely the work of the clergy. The Protestants were only able to be successful, however, because of the

By the start of the 16th century the Catholic Church contained many with reforming ideas, but Martin Luther was perhaps unusual in the degree to which he was prepared to take his opposition to ecclesiastical authority. In 1508, he became a professor at the newly founded University of Wittenberg, and apart from a brief interlude when he was in Rome for the Augustinian Order, of which he was a member, he retained his position there until his death in 1546. Here, in a mid-century representation by Lucas Cranach the Elder, he is shown preaching in Wittenberg parish church.

patronage of lay rulers – the endorsement and protection of the 'Godly Princes' who recognized the value of the religious changes for the promotion of national and dynastic ambition. *Cuius regio, eius religio* – the religion of the prince is the religion of the country – was a maxim that had adhered the support of the feudal kingdoms to the Catholic Church at the end of the Roman world; now, in the sixteenth century, it became the basis of the Protestant Reformation. The ancient notion of a universal society had been in decline in the later Middle Ages anyway, and as kings throughout Europe gained in personal authority at the expense of the feudal magnates, and consolidated dynastic loyalties around coherent territorial entities, the Church more or less alone remained outside their control. Where they had imposed their authority, as in the appointment of clergy in the proprietary churches they had endowed, there had always been a potential for conflict with papal authority, as the Investiture Controversy had shown.

In the later Middle Ages royal power increasingly regulated economic activity, and kings expected their subjects to owe loyalty on the basis of national identity; this allowed reasons of state rather than religious identity to define international relations. The entire debate about papal claims to temporal authority was marginalized by the emergence of the nation state. For the Church was, *de facto*, no longer a universal spiritual empire: it was losing ground, and that rapidly, to the actions of the monarchies in their control of ever more extensive dimensions of national life. There is a sense in which the revival of papal claims in the fifteenth century was not only an indication of its recovery from the humiliations of the fourteenth, but also a reaction to the growing emancipation of secular power in most parts of western Europe. Many of the medieval institutions which had provided the structures to which the Catholic Church had addressed its mission were being wrecked by the emergence of the nation states; representative bodies, though not the rule of law, were being subordinated to princely ambition.

Only in England under the Tudor dynasty did parliamentary institutions continue to evolve in anything but a highly formal manner.

Originally, the papacy had been the successor of the sovereignty of the Roman emperors, in the sense that the popes claimed universal religious authority and were subject to no external power on earth. Now the European monarchs were claiming the same kind of sovereignty, though limited to the boundaries of each nation state. They were the new successors of the Roman concept of authority – a legacy of Roman imperial practice embodied in Roman law. Their assertion of autonomy was bound to have implications in religious matters, especially since so many commonplace issues in each of their states were subject to ecclesiastical canon law and not to their own judicial systems: issues such as marriage discipline, oaths, and the transfer of capital to fund the central operations of the Catholic Church. Around such considerations grievances accumulated, and the materials for what became the Protestant Reformation stacked up in each country. Martin Luther realized that only the protection and endorsement of the princes would enable a separation from Rome – a break that would bring about the implementation of the religious reforms he and others sought, alongside the assertion of national sovereignty to which the princes aspired.

It was according to this coincidence of interests that the map of the Reformation, and the division of the Catholic south and the Protestant north, was drawn. Spain and France had made separate concordats with Rome, and so achieved a practical control of the internal conduct of the Catholic Church in those countries. England and the German states had not, and they separated from historic Christendom in the Reformation. The parliament of Henry VIII in England, in legislating against appeals to Rome in 1534, declared that the realm of England was 'an empire' – that it was sovereign and autonomous. But the general ideals of the religious reform movement remained broadly present, whatever the outcome of the Reformation split. Spain and France remained inside the Catholic Church, yet in 1564 Philip II of Spain only accepted the decrees of the Council of Trent conditionally (if they did not infringe the royal prerogative), and in 1615 France declined to guarantee their implementation by the clergy. Whether a nation remained Catholic, or joined the Protestant secession, therefore, did not alter the overall change in the balance of *sacerdotium* and *imperium*. Catholic states persisted in reserving their independent prerogatives. The nation-states had shown that they did not need the authority of the Church to legitimize their exercise of power. The modern world was being created.

It is unclear how widespread dissatisfaction with the condition of the Catholic Church was on the eve of the Reformation. Certainly the changes made by the Protestants – Lutheran or Calvinist – were not in themselves inspired by popular movements; they were also urban rather than rural, a

Henry VIII, King of England, surrounded by his family: a panel of *c.*1590–5 after Lucas de Heere. Henry's policy of conservative religious reform, accompanied by extensive seizure of ecclesiastical property, was not unusual among the Catholic monarchs of early modern Europe, but his break from Roman authority placed England unavoidably within the Protestant camp.

triumph of the educated classes over the peasantry of the countryside. Religious fervour among the population generally does not seem to have been in decline at the end of the Middle Ages. Indeed, it was producing some luxuriant growths, including a flowering of mysticism, and the production of a popular devotional literature. Lollardy was inspired by the Englishman John Wycliffe, who died in 1384. His pursuit of simplicity in theology – he was an Oxford academic – attracted numerous heretical ideas in England and in Bohemia. There is a tendency to judge Lollardy as the only sign of popular religion, to ignore the continuing mass veneration of religious images, and to suppose that the phenomenon of popular spirituality was an inevitable precursor of Protestantism. Subsequent Protestant polemical writing and preaching encouraged such conclusions. But if anything it was the Protestant changes, representing the will of minorities of clergy and public men, which were resented, as the old familiar rites were abolished and the churches were sanitized of their traditional images of the saints.

The scandals and abuses of the Catholic Church were not, in fact, by the standards of the times, particularly scandalous or abusive; their equivalents were abundantly available in the lay world of affairs. Yet men of considered judgement were appalled by what they saw – as the finer spirits in every age

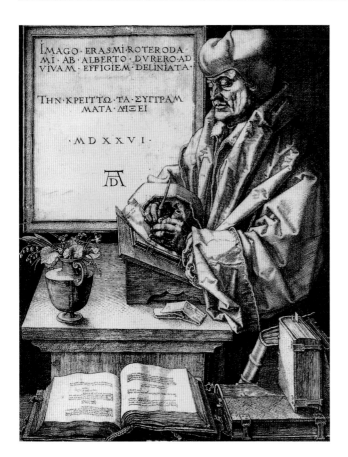

ABOVE Erasmus of Rotterdam was acknowledged as the greatest scholar of the first half of the 16th century, and in his polemical writings he also revealed himself as a radical reformer of the Church. He remained a Catholic. This portrayal is by Albrecht Dürer.

OPPOSITE Erasmus settled in Basle in 1514 and there produced his great translation of the Greek New Testament. This page shows the beginning of St Matthew's Gospel, with Erasmus's Latin version printed next to the Greek text.

have been when the splendour of Christ's message is contrasted with the fearful compromises and worldliness that humans impose upon the divine materials at the disposal of the Church. Institutions, however, were often not easy to shift, especially in a social culture that regarded office-holding as a species of property, where ties of loyalty were still quasi-feudal, and where family or dynastic interests were invested in ecclesiastical employment.

By the start of the sixteenth century there was something like a consensus for reform among the educated classes. The writings of Erasmus – who when he died in 1536 was recognized as the most famous scholar of the age – included some biting criticisms of the unreformed Church. The most widely disseminated of these were in the *Praise of Folly*, published in 1509 while he was living in England, and in the even more influential *Enchiridion Militis Christiani* (*Manual of the Christian Knight*) of 1504. Erasmus had been educated by the Brethren of the Common Life at their school in Deventer in the Low Countries. This monastic association of men, among whose members were Thomas à Kempis, author of *The Imitation of Christ* (c.1427), sought a revival of Biblicism in the Church, and encouraged the growing enthusiasm for popular devotions. Erasmus was a Greek scholar who settled in Basle in 1514. There he produced his famous translation of the Greek New Testament into Latin (and thereby exhibited deficiencies in the official Vulgate of St Jerome). He was regarded with suspicion by both Catholic and Protestants, and his works were for a time proscribed by Paul IV. But his sharp observations of abuses in the Church – he was an archetypal don – merely expressed in intellectual language opinions that were extremely widely entertained.

Distaste for the low living evidently characteristic of some of the lower clergy, and of high living by the hierarchy, was self-explanatory: a steady-state of criticism of the sort had hedged the Church since the time of Constantine. Some abuses need more considered explanation because they constituted the new material of the polemicism of the Reformation. The institutionalized avoidance of Catholic teaching on usury was an obvious inconsistency, especially since trading practices, the emergence of middle-class entrepreneurs and adventurers, the need, even among senior clerics, to raise money on loan to pay the fees for entry into office, and numerous

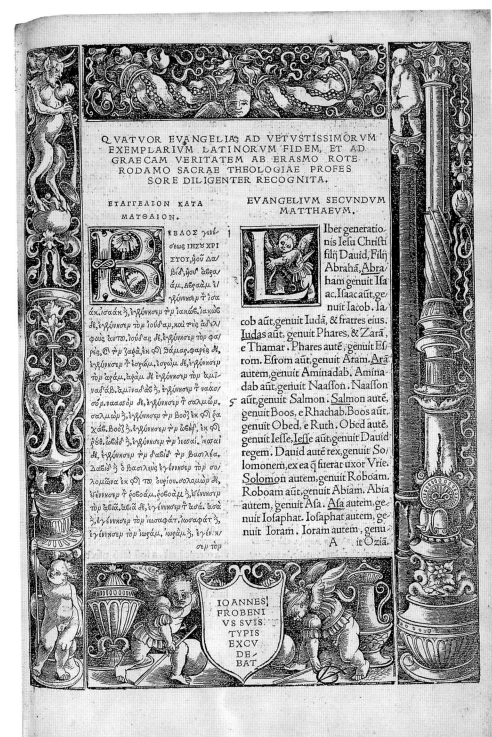

QVATVOR EVANGELIA, AD VETVSTISSIMORVM
EXEMPLARIVM LATINORVM FIDEM, ET AD
GRAECAM VERITATEM AB ERASMO ROTE
RODAMO SACRAE THEOLOGIAE PROFES
SORE DILIGENTER RECOGNITA.

ΕΥΑΓΓΕΛΙΟΝ ΚΑΤΑ
ΜΑΤΘΑΙΟΝ.

ΒΙΒΛΟΣ γενέ
σεως ΙΗΣΥ ΧΡΙ
ΣΤΟΥ, ἡοῦ Δα
βίδ, ἡοῦ ἀβρα
άμ. ἀβραάμ ἐ
γέννησεν τ᾿ ἰσα
άκ. ἰσαὰκ δ᾽, ἐγέννησεν τὸν ἰακώβ. ἰακώβ
δὲ, ἐγέννησεν τὸν ἰούδαμ, καὶ τοὺς ἀδελ
φοὺς αυτω. ἰούδας δὲ, ἐγέννησεν τὸν φα
ρὲς, ὅ τὸν ζαρὰ, ἐκ τᾶ θάμας. φαρὲς δὲ,
ἐγέννησεν τ᾿ ἐσρώμ. ἐσρὼμ δὲ, ἐγέννησεν
τὸν ἀράμ. ἀρὰμ δὲ ἐγέννησεν τὸν ἀμι
ναδ᾽άβ. ἀμιναδὰβ δὲ, ἐγέννησεν τ᾿ νάασ᾽
σόμ. νάασσόμ δὲ, ἐγέννησεν τ᾿ σαλμώμ,
σαλμὼμ δὲ, ἐγέννησεν τὸμ βοὸζ ἐκ τᾶ ῥα
χάβ. βοὸζ δὲ, ἐγέννησεν τὸμ ὠβὴδ, ἐκ τᾶ
ῥὔθ. ὠβὴδ δὲ, ἐγέννησεν τὸμ ἰεσαί. ἰεσαὶ
δὲ, ἐγέννησεν τὸμ δαβίδ τὸμ βασιλέα.
δαβὶδ δὲ ὁ βασιλεὺς ἐγέννησεν τὸμ σο
λομῶνα ἐκ τῆ τῶ οὐρίου. σολομὼμ δὲ,
ἐγέννησεν τ᾿ ῥοβοάμ. ῥοβοὰμ δὲ, ἐγέννησεν
τὸμ ἀβιᾶ. ἀβιᾶ δὲ, ἐγέννησεμ τ᾿ ἀσά. ἀσὰ
δὲ, ἐγέννησεν τὸμ ἰωσαφάτ. ἰωσαφάτ δὲ,
ἐγέννησεν τὸμ ἰωράμ. ἰωρὰμ δὲ, ἐγέν. ἦ
σεμ τὸμ

EVANGELIVM SECVNDVM
MATTHAEVM.

Iber generatio
nis Iesu Christi
filij Dauid, Filij
Abrahã, Abra
ham genuit Isa
ac. Isaac aũt, ge
nuit Iacob. Ia
cob aũt, genuit Iudã, & fratres eius.
Iudas aũt, genuit Phares, & Zarã,
e Thamar. Phares autẽ, genuit Es
rom. Esrom aũt, genuit Aram. Arã
autem, genuit Aminadab. Amina
dab aũt, genuit Naasson. Naasson
5 aũt, genuit Salmon. Salmon autẽ,
genuit Boos, e Rhachab. Boos aũt,
genuit Obed, e Ruth. Obed autẽ,
genuit Iesse. Iesse aũt, genuit Dauid
regem. Dauid autẽ rex, genuit So/
lomonem, ex ea q̃ fuerat uxor Vrie.
Solomon autem, genuit Roboam.
Roboam aũt, genuit Abiam. Abiã
autem, genuit Asa. Asa autem, ge
nuit Iosaphat. Iosaphat autem, ge
nuit Ioram. Ioram autem, genu
A   it Ozíã.

IOANNES
FROBENI
VS SVIS
TYPIS
EXCV
DE
BAT

other effects of the rise of banking, especially in Italian and German free cities, all conspired to place the ban on the taking of usury on the reformers' lists. This was done, it must be added, with very little hope of abolition, but more in order to show up clerical practices. 'He that takes usury goes to hell,' as Benvenuto da Imola wrote in the fourteenth century, 'and he who takes none is on the brink of bankruptcy.'

Usury had been formally condemned at the Third Lateran Council in 1179 – a ban not lifted until 1745 by Benedict XIV. It was not observed, seemingly, by anyone, since ways around it were numerous. Aquinas and the schoolmen had been vehemently opposed to usury, citing Exodus, Deuteronomy and Aristotle, as authorities. Some rationalization of the Church's teaching, despite the unanimity of the Scriptures and the doctors of the Church, was plainly necessary. The Reformation did not supply it, at least in the short-term, in either the Catholic or the Protestant Churches, but the issue itself considerably assisted the general sense that Christian institutions were out of touch with actual practice among believers.

Indeed, money was a sensitive matter in other ways, especially in the payment of taxes to Rome, and in the greatly satirised question of indulgences – a by-product of the Crusades, which had in part been financed through the sale of hire-purchase redemption. More important than all this, however, was the ill will among the laity caused by the ecclesiastical laws on marriage. Matrimonial litigation was the most frequent and most complicated issue before the Church courts. It was, of course, Clement VII's (rather flexible, as it happened) dealings over King Henry VIII's matrimonial status in 1530 that precipitated religious change in England. There was not in Church law – as there is not to this day – any provision for divorce. *Divortium*, in the courts, meant nullity or separation. Impediments leading to nullity were customarily due to accidental consanguinity: in overwhelmingly small rural societies it was quite easy to contract a marriage with a relative within the prohibited table of affinity compiled out of Mosaic law.

To compound matters, marriages were virtually all arranged, among all classes, with material settlements very much to the fore: this was before romantic notions of human love had much to do with marriage, and when life expectancy was anyway short so that errors in the liaison were unlikely to produce very long-lasting misery. Boys, however, could marry at the age of fourteen and girls at twelve; this lengthened marriage slightly. In the frequent legal proceedings consequent on marriage failure, the Church courts had to proceed with circumspection, to avoid conflict with Roman law and with the unwritten customs of feudal society. Lengthy appeals to Rome, for those who could afford them, often resulted. So did considerable confusion. The irritating outcome was the accumulation of complications in the relations of Church officials with individuals in society. They explain why

The complications of canon law in relation to marital questions were a cause of unpopularity for ecclesiastical authority. In closely-knit rural societies, however, accidental marriages within family relationships could quite easily be contracted when the rules were unclear. Hence the production of tables of consanguinity showing the degrees of kinship. This example is German, *c.*1300.

Erasmus wrote his tract *The Institution of Christian Marriage* in 1526, and why the Council of Trent formally decreed what the Church had anyway taught informally for centuries – that marriage is a sacrament – thus hoping to elevate the whole tone of the question.

The accessibility of the Bible had been a major incentive in the appeal of the Lollards; in the reforming pressures of the sixteenth century it assumed

something near to predominance. The Latin Vulgate, authorized by the Holy See, was plainly defective in accuracy as a translation, as the Greek scholarship of the Christian Humanists was now able to demonstrate. In the intellectual world, in fact, a kind of consensus came into existence about the need for a new text: this prevailed both among those who were secure in Catholic ecclesiology and those who were to join the Protestant secessions. It is not difficult to see why papal authorities were so cautious, since medieval heresy had been eaten up with erroneous, and sometimes bizarre, understandings of the Scriptures. There was a widely held belief that access to biblical knowledge would show incompatibilities with traditional Church teaching. Even sophisticated thinkers such as Marsiglio of Padua cited Scripture in order to deny papal claims.

The appearance of popular spiritual works in the vernacular during the later Middle Ages – like the mystical writings of the Lady Julian of Norwich, and popular accounts of the life of St Catherine of Siena – indicated the growth of a public taste, at least among the minority who were literate, for religious information. Even before Luther published his German version of the New Testament, in 1522, there were already fourteen translations of the Bible in German and four in Dutch. It was the printing press that ended Rome's policy of exclusive adhesion to the Latin Bible: Europe was flooded with unauthorized versions of the Scriptures. The 'Open Bible' came to be seen by Protestants as a distinctly Protestant achievement, and with some truth; but it was Erasmus's work with the Greek texts, and the university scholarship of the Christian Humanists, which enabled an equally central place for the advance of biblical learning within the Catholic Church itself. The papacy looked on nervously, adhering, still, to the work of St Jerome.

Many of the accusations of abuses directed against the Catholic Church were familiar enough repetitions of the internal exhortations to reform that had been heard periodically for several centuries. There was both truth and exaggeration in most of them. At the centre of the assault on the corruptions of the monastic life, with which the Protestant activists infused the popular religious culture of the territories where they were successful, were arguments for reform which had been made by monastic reformers themselves. Institutions that had a European-wide distribution, often with centralized direction, free of episcopal control, and under the direct patronage of the Holy See, were not, in point of fact, all that easy to reform. Local variations and local differences in the nature of endowment existed everywhere, despite the apparent uniformities. Securing changes in which all the dispersed houses of a particular order moved together was not easily managed. Secular lords and, later, merchant entrepreneurs, had endowed some houses, and could not always see the advantage of disruptions to the

stability of the religious world in which they had invested. Tithes were a perpetual grievance; sometimes they were paid to monks who might even live in another country. The wealth of some of the houses also attracted the attention of the princes, who recognized in them a useful annex to their treasuries. The dissolution of the monasteries and chantries which accompanied the Protestant upheaval, however, should be judged in the context of existing Catholic practice – of more or less permanent spasms of monastic reform, in which the suppression of houses was not uncommon.

The outpouring of hostile criticism which initiated the Protestant revolt also produced the foundation of numerous new orders in the Catholic Church, from the later years of the fifteenth century – such as the Oratory of Divine Love, founded at Genoa in 1497, or the Theatines, started in Rome in 1524, or the Barnabites, founded in Milan in 1530. In orders like these were found, once again, the ancient appeal for a return to the simplicity of life and the evangelistic zeal of the original monastic vocation. They also addressed themselves to a wider world, and were in this sense precursors of the great missionary orders of the Counter Reformation.

Attitudes to the Reformation in later centuries tended to be influenced by the propaganda put out in England at the time, for England became the leading Protestant state and the national enemy of Spain – which was the most powerful of the European countries in the sixteenth century, seat of a great empire and of the 'Most Catholic' sovereigns, the secular bulwark of the Catholic Church. Protestantism in England developed an interpretation of Spanish Catholicism that over time became the customary way in which the English-speaking world evaluated the Catholic Church. Popular anti-Catholic sentiment became an essential ingredient in English national identity and, at times, a useful political cohesive. It was a tradition of thinking which not surprisingly chose to ignore the existence within Spanish Catholicism of an influential reformist movement. The leading advocate was Cardinal Francisco Ximénez de Cisneros, Archbishop of Toledo, the primatial see of Spain. He was a friar, noted for simplicity of living and a desire to purify the Church of corruption. The University of Alcalá, which he founded and endowed, attracted distinguished scholars from Paris, Bologna and Salamanca. As Regent of Spain during the minority, in 1516, of Charles I of Castile (later the Emperor Charles V), he was influential in the formation of the Spanish monarchy at a time of crucial consolidation – and therefore a powerful voice in the emergence of Spanish sponsorship of Catholic reform in the sixteenth century. He died in 1517. English opinion about Spanish practice in the Counter Reformation, however, was fashioned in ignorance of its reform tradition. English popular anti-papal sentiment, which endured to the end of the nineteenth century, and beyond, was dependent on what it represented as the horrible crimes of the priests. There evolved a 'No Popery' litany, with references supplied by the publication of John Foxe's *Book of Martyrs* in 1563, the excommunication of Queen Elizabeth I by St Pius V in the bull *Regnans in Excelsis* of 1570, and the Armada sent by Spain to recover England for Catholicism in 1588.

But the Catholic institution that above all others appeared to embody the reality of Catholic authoritarianism, the inherent incompatibility of papalism and liberty, was the Inquisition – always referred to as the *Spanish* Inquisition, although it existed in many Catholic countries. To this day, liberal opinion imagines the Inquisition as conclusive proof of the unenlightened and cruel nature of Catholicism at the time of the Reformation. The fact is that it existed in another time, and its preoccupation with the extirpation of wrong beliefs is simply not conducive to modern understanding of religion. The concept of evil has become secularized; modern tribunals are concerned with genocide, not with the prospects of eternal life.

The *auto da fe*; a late 17th-century French version of the proceedings of the Inquisition in Spain. Protestant polemicism, and extravagant descriptions of the Inquisition, have given it a permanent place in anti-Catholic tradition.

In 1233, Gregory IX appointed permanent papal Inquisitors, most of whom were Franciscan and Dominican friars, to prosecute heresy. The Inquisitors had no powers except spiritual ones; heretics who recanted were given ordinary penances – usually those dispensed in the confessional. Heretics who were obdurate were handed over to the secular authorities and were punished according to the laws of each city or state. This was a code of procedure more or less uniform across Europe. The consequences were not, in reality, especially draconian, especially when set against the normal fearsome administration of punishment in the Middle Ages. Heretics were executed by burning; conventional criminals were usually hung. In the middle of the thirteenth century, at the height of the Albigensian campaign, some three people a year were being executed for heresy. What first brought the Inquisition tribunals into disrepute was their use by King Philip IV of France in his brutal suppression of the Templars in the fourteenth century: it was the secular, not the religious, authority that was largely responsible.

In the fifteenth century the Inquisition was reformed by Paul III, seeking to bring the proceedings under closer centralized control. This had the unforeseen effect, however, of associating the Inquisition more directly with papal authority itself. In Spain, at the same time, the monarchy employed the Inquisition tribunals to stamp out irregular beliefs and practice among converted Moors and Jews, using inquisitorial methods inherited from the preceding Islamic heresy courts. Hence the new Spanish Inquisition of 1480, of which, in 1483, Tomás de Torquemada became Inquisitor General. Though both he, and the tribunals, were unmistakably instruments of Crown policy, subsequent Protestant propaganda for centuries identified the entire Catholic Church in Spain, and elsewhere, with their occasional excesses.

By the nineteenth century political liberals and religious dissenters took the 'crimes' of the Inquisition to be ultimate proofs of the vile character of 'popery', and an enormous popular literature on the subject poured from the presses of Europe and North America. At its most active, in the sixteenth century, nevertheless, the Inquisition was regarded as far more enlightened than the secular courts: if you denied the Trinity and repented you were given a penance; if you stole a sheep and repented you were hung. It has

been calculated that only one per cent of those who appeared before Inquisition tribunals eventually received death penalties. But the damage wrought by propaganda has been effective, and today the 'Spanish' Inquisition, like the Crusades, persists in supplying supposedly discreditable episodes to damn the memory of the Catholic past.

The Spanish monarchy may have been the material guardian of the Counter Reformation but it was the Jesuits who were its spiritual activists, inheriting, in effect, the role formerly filled by the Orders of Military Knights. In 1534, St Ignatius Loyola and six friends studying, as he was, in Paris, took a vow of poverty and service to others; in 1540, they were formally constituted as the Society of Jesus in the bull *Regimini Militantis Ecclesiae*. Ignatius became its first General. In 1541, he published the *Spiritual Exercises*, a manual for retreat directors: the new mission laid out its priorities of personal spiritual formation and evangelistic advance. Ignatius had originally intended charitable and evangelistic work among the Islamic people of the Holy Land, where he had earlier been on pilgrimage, and there was something of the afterglow of the Crusading ideal in the Jesuit missionary vision. By the time of his death in 1556 there were already a thousand members of the Society.

In a painting of 1641–2, Pope Urban VIII, surrounded by cardinals, visits the Gesù during the celebrations of the centenary of the Society of Jesus.

The Jesuits contained a robust intellectual element, which became notable for defence of papal claims and for assisting the reforms of the Council of Trent. The papalist sympathies of the Society, in fact, quite early attracted opposition within the Church, and this was to remain as a permanent feature of their history. Their anti-monarchical contentions, eloquently and systematically articulated, were particularly unwelcome to some in France; Spain was by then the protector of the papacy. French troops, indeed, had sacked Rome in 1527. It was the influence of the crowns which helped to procure the suppression of the Jesuits (or temporary removal, as it turned out) towards the end of the eighteenth century. The Jesuits realized that the old tensions of pope and emperor no longer represented the realities of sixteenth-century Europe. Organic concepts of empire and universal claims of allegiance had passed: Europe was a continent of independent nation-states. The Reformation occurred *after* this enormous shift in the balance of things had taken place – it was itself a symptom of the new world order. The Jesuits, in effect, assisted the Counter Reformation Catholic Church to readjust its strategic overview, to accommodate the new conditions, and to draw lines in the sand.

The leading Jesuit exponent of the resulting neo-papalism was St Robert Bellarmine, a Tuscan who joined the Society in 1560, and spent his life from

1576 in the Collegium Romanum. His emphatic papalism earned him the execration of Protestants: his features were caricatured, in appliqué rosettes, on the salt-glaze jugs made in the Low Countries in the seventeenth century and popularly known, reasonably enough, as 'Bellarmine jugs'. Yet he was actually a convinced reformer, openly sympathetic to Galileo, and to the ideal of an accessible Bible. In 1592, he took a leading part in the revision of the Vulgate. His theory of papalism, most extensively expounded in the *Disputationes*, published in three volumes between 1586 and 1593, accepted that the papacy made no claims to secular authority. As spiritual head of the Church, however, with powers that came directly from God, the pope had a superior authority to that of the monarchs, whose powers derived from God only indirectly. Subjects had no absolute duty of obedience to secular rulers; the pope was possessed, in fact, of the right to release them from their obligation of obedience if spiritualities were infringed. Popes may depose heretical rulers.

If this doctrine is added to Francisco Suárez's view, expounded in the later years of the sixteenth century, that the state is of purely natural origin, and that whereas states are national the Church is universal, the indirect right of the pope to control the spiritual destinies of human society has an inclusive consistency. Suárez was a Spanish Jesuit; he had moved some way,

ABOVE Cardinal Bellarmine, a Jesuit and a leading reformer of the Catholic Church in the second half of the 16th century, put the Decrees of the Council of Trent into effect. This attracted the obloquy of Protestants, who attempted to ridicule the cardinal by moulding caricature likenesses of his face on the necks of salt-glaze jugs. 'Bellarmine' jugs of this design were very common in the 17th century.

RIGHT In Protestant countries the practice of Catholicism was often outside the law, and this meant that gatherings of the clergy had to be held discreetly and sometimes at personal risk. Here is a Catholic consultation in England in 1620, under the Stuart monarchy, when Catholics received a degree of official toleration.

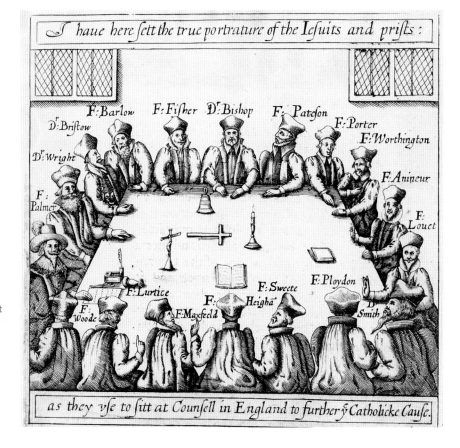

in these ideas, from the actual conduct of the Spanish Crown in controlling the affairs of the Church in the dominions at home and in the colonial empire. Such expressions of the right of subjects to rebel against heretical rulers lodged in the collective memory of Protestantism. It explains the special horror of 'Jesuitry' to be found in subsequent popular Protestantism.

The overseas Jesuit missions were a spearhead in the extension of Catholicism in the sixteenth and seventeenth centuries; this, and the extraordinary vision of St Francis Xavier, will be assessed in the next chapter. But in Europe itself the Society founded large numbers of schools and colleges, and established a kind of Jesuit brand of intellectual excellence. They also encouraged the preaching of missions inside European countries, intended to re-energize and rededicate the Catholic populations. The sixteenth century saw a further round in the establishment of religious orders, many of which had domestic mission as their leading purpose, combined with works of social welfare. These foundations were not really reactions to the Protestant secessions; some had begun before Luther's public questioning of authority, and others were, in effect, indistinguishable from the types of monastic reform that had given vitality to the late medieval Church. Like them, they tended to be designed to operate in the world and not in the cloister, and the vows taken were accordingly linked to service and activism, and to education, rather than to the purely contemplative life.

St Vincent de Paul, founder of the Lazarist Fathers, and of the Sisters of Charity (together with St Louise de Marillac) in 1633. He also did much to alleviate the conditions of prisoners and to encourage missions among country people in France. In 1638, he set up the first organization of homes for orphans: foundlings are here shown being cared for by one of the Sisters of Charity.

Thus, for example, the Discalced Carmelites founded in 1562 by St Teresa of Avila, in central Spain, aimed at the restoration of Carmelite austerity in order to establish a dedicated basis for service in the world – a balance that reflected the nature of Teresa herself, a mystic and a practical reformer. The Capuchins, a reformed Franciscan order instituted in 1529 by Matteo di Bassi at Urbino in Italy, were active preachers and missioners. Or there was the Congregation of the Oratory, set up in Rome by St Philip Neri and approved by Gregory XIII in 1575. It was a community of priests who undertook work among the sick and the poor; Neri himself achieved a reputation for sanctity and judgement which extended to giving advice to popes and cardinals. St Francis de Sales, Bishop of Geneva from 1602, founded the Visitation Sisters with St Jane Frances de Chantal, for the promotion of charitable and

ABOVE St Philip Neri, founder of the Oratorians, an order approved by Gregory XIII in 1575. A marble statue at Santa Maria in Vallicella, Rome. It was to this order that Newman and Manning were admitted after their adhesion to the Catholic faith in 19th-century England.

ABOVE RIGHT St Francis de Sales, by Carlo Maratta, was Bishop of Geneva early in the 17th century. He gazes upwards to receive a vision of the Virgin and the celestial society.

OPPOSITE St Teresa of Avila by Gianlorenzo Bernini, at Santa Maria della Vittoria in Rome, 1645–52. She was the embodiment of Spanish Counter Reformation spirituality.

missionary services. These, and many other orders and associations, were the practical means of spreading the ideals of the Counter Reformation to the Catholic populations.

The spiritual energy of sixteenth-century Catholicism was unquestionably challenged by the Protestant Reformation, and the fracturing of the religious unity of western Europe. But its inherent vitality can be recognized in what was the most far-reaching of its achievements – the Council of Trent. The Canons and Decrees of the Council were a blueprint for the reform of the Church, for centralized direction operating through a revitalized diocesan structure. Catholic teaching in faith and morals was expressed according to Tridentine formulae for the next three centuries, and beyond. In the nineteenth century popular Protestant writers and orators were still assailing the Council of Trent as the great example of Rome at its most authoritarian.

When Paul III called the nineteenth General Council of the Church in 1542 it was clear that general reform was the end in view: Cardinal Contarini headed a group of reformers whose ideas furnished the agenda. There were,

however, hazards. The Emperor Charles V favoured a council, and despite the ancient tradition of imperial participation in councils of the Church, and Charles's presumed benign intentions, it could not be assumed that the gathering would avoid being utilized for the promotion of Spanish policy. Attempts by the popes to summon councils in 1537 and 1538 had not succeeded – but then Charles V had not favoured them. By 1545, when the first session opened at Trent, the threat from advanced reformers who were seemingly prepared to break the unity of the Church was clear. Another risk for the papacy came from the conciliar themes that had been advanced at the Council of Constance in 1415. Luther, in 1518, sought to appeal to the authority of a General Council over the authority of the pope.

In the event, the Council of Trent avoided the dangers, and the three sessions, of 1545–7, 1551–2 and 1562–3, laid the foundations of the modern papacy, and clarified the essentials of Catholic teaching in a manner that drew clear lines between Catholic orthodoxy and the beliefs and practices of the Protestant secessionists. Its definitions and formulae touch an enormous range of Catholic teaching and discipline. At the second session, those Protestants who still attended argued for the supremacy of General Councils over the authority of the papacy, but for the last time. The first session had laid out and sanctioned the Catholic belief that the authority of the church derived from both Scripture and Tradition: a denial of the exclusive Biblicism that defined Protestantism. Yet a reform of the text of the Vulgate was also ordered (and completed in 1592). The seven sacraments were specified as necessary doctrinal rites. The doctrine of Transubstantiation – the corporeal presence of Christ in the Mass – was confirmed at the second session, and at the third, convoked by Pius IV in 1562, the sacrificial nature of the Mass was defined more precisely.

This last session also made numerous detailed provisions to regulate and centralize the Church, providing institutions for its ordinary operations and for its expansion. By that time the Protestant secessions had accomplished what was beginning to look like a permanent schism. In the Catholic Church there remained some differences of emphasis between the Italian bishops, who tended to insist on the exclusive spiritual authority of the pope, and the Spanish bishops, many of whom harboured residual inclinations to regard the authority of bishops as equally derived directly from God. But the actual business of the third session of the Council was contoured by the Jesuit theologians. The bureaucracy of the Church was radically reformed – and some very long-standing abuses, such as the length of proceedings in matrimonial courts, were abolished in a revised code of procedures. Some practices which had initiated past scandals were subject to new regulations: indulgences, the invocation of saints and the veneration of relics. Provision was made for more preaching by parish clergy. The standards of

OPPOSITE The Council of Trent established extensive regulations about the conduct of worship, requiring universality of practice. The Tridentine Mass remained the form familiar to most participants and observers until the changes stipulated at the Second Vatican Council in 1962. It was this ritual which, to many Protestants, seemed, erroneously, to be the defining feature of Catholic Christianity.

the priesthood were to be elevated by the establishment of diocesan seminaries; bishops were to be appointed according to procedures approved by Rome; there were to be regular provincial and diocesan synods. The Decrees of the Council of Trent were confirmed by Pius IV in 1564. It had been an extraordinary triumph, achieved in the most difficult of circumstances.

The ferment of reform – for it was no other – received ecclesiastical structure in the great pontificate of St Pius V, who ascended the papal throne in 1566. He was a Dominican friar; indeed the subsequent papal custom of wearing a white cassock is said to derive from Pius V's preference for his white Dominican habit. He was a conscientious reformer, and used the Decrees of Trent as his guidelines – as expressed in the Roman Catechism of 1566. He also revised the Breviary and the Missal. His principal assistant, and by any standards an administrator of extraordinary energy, was St Charles Borromeo, a nobleman from northern Italy who was Archbishop of Milan from 1566. Pius V had a declared distaste for the nepotism of his predecessor; Borromeo, as it happened, was actually Pius IV's nephew. He had a huge influence in the last session of the Council, and through the implementation of its reforms in his own province gave an example that was extensively followed. In Rome itself Pius V assisted the establishment of national colleges for students from each country. He also ruled that bishops throughout the Church should undertake periodic *ad limina* visits to Rome to give an account of the territories under their supervision. This arrangement gave the Vatican a wider and deeper range of knowledge of world conditions, both then and thereafter, than has been available to other governments. Missionary areas, in what was projected as a universal evangelistic campaign, came under the Sacred Congregation *de Propaganda Fide* (for the Propagation of the Faith) in Rome. The papal curia itself – the administrative service – was reformed, and the other Congregations bureaucratized. In 1588, Sixtus V authorized fifteen permanent Congregations, each under the direction of a Cardinal-Prefect. The number of cardinals itself was fixed at seventy.

What the papacy had created, under the inspiration of the Tridentine Decrees, was a centralized bureaucracy which was to last until the next council in 1869. The changes spread out from Rome; everywhere there was a renewed attention to Christian works. Everywhere, additionally, there was a more systematic attention to education – headed by the new teaching orders – which blew away many of the last superstitions of the medieval world. Less magic adhered to the understanding of the faith in rural churches, and there was more learning in their pastors. The lines in this shift of understanding should not be drawn too decisively, however: ideas from the old world lingered on. There was much attention to education in the new Protestant churches, too, and yet popular superstition survived

OPPOSITE St Charles Borromeo, by Orazio Borgianni, *c.*1610–16. It was Borromeo who, as Archbishop of Milan after 1566, gave an example of how to implement the Canons and Decrees of the Council of Trent – an example widely emulated throughout the Catholic world.

ABOVE At the sea battle of Lepanto, in the entrance to the Gulf of Corinth in 1571, a Catholic alliance defeated the Turkish fleet and achieved naval supremacy in the Mediterranean. The removal, at least at sea, of further Islamic advances was greeted with exultation throughout Europe. In the Catholic Church the victory is still observed today as the celebration of the Rosary. This depiction of the battle is by Hendrick Vroom the Younger.

OPPOSITE ABOVE Pope Julius II, by Raphael, c.1511. Giuliano della Rovere ascended the papal throne in 1503, and was most notable for restoring and enlarging the States of the Church in Italy, and thereby protecting the independence of the papacy, and of the Church, from external political interference. He also sought to end the practice of simony in the Church. He is most remembered today, however, as a great patron of the arts.

there as well. It was the Puritans who burned witches, and the French Catholics who in 1572 succumbed to the popular hysteria which resulted in the Massacre of St Bartholomew's Day, in which some thousands of French Protestants were slaughtered.

The Counter Reformation was in reality a 'normal' development; its reforms grew out of late medieval ideas and were given shape and system in a Europe created by the rise of the nation-states. Something like the Council of Trent would have occurred regardless of Henry VIII's marital difficulties or Luther's theses. The bureaucratization of the Roman curia in effect imparted some of the characteristics of the new monarchies to the Catholic Church itself. The pope was becoming a ruler among other rulers in Europe, the head of a sovereign state in Italy with the same problems of government experienced everywhere. The States of the Church were conducted according to principles and practices that differed little from those of the new national governments, Catholic or Protestant. The evolving world order had a certain uniformity, as medieval institutions and social organizations slipped away into obsolescence.

Two events, one strategic and one symbolical, defined the way in which the sixteenth century opened the Catholic Church to the modern world. In 1565, the siege of Malta by the Ottomans under Suleiman the Magnificent was lifted. The home of the Knights Hospitaller was saved; but the threat to Christendom itself had not diminished. At the entrance to the Gulf of

Corinth in 1571 the 'Christian League', inspired by Pius V with Spain and Venice, defeated the Turks in the great naval battle of Lepanto. The Mediterranean was once again safe for Christian shipping, and although the Ottoman Turks remained at the gates of Vienna the universal threat from Islam had been rolled back. The Pope declared a thanksgiving feast of Our Lady, to be observed in October each year: it exists to this day as the celebration of the Rosary.

Another defining event was the building of a new basilica over the tomb of St Peter in Rome. Julius II had in 1506 decided on the radical project: Constantine's old church was dismantled, and in 1593 a great new basilica, designed in part by Michelangelo, was completed. Its baroque splendour, classical grace and colossal scale – it was the largest structure built since Antiquity – have made it the most immediately recognizable church in the world. It has become the symbol of Catholic Christianity.

RIGHT In 1506, Pope Julius II ordered the dismantling of Constantine's basilica of St Peter's in Rome – raised above the tomb of the apostle – and the rebuilding of a grand new church. After a succession of architects and artists had worked on the design, including Michelangelo, the new St Peter's was completed by 1593. It remains the most splendid and well-known symbol of the Catholic faith.

OVERLEAF The interior of St Peter's basilica, as depicted by Giovanni Pannini in the 18th century. The seated statue of St Peter (see page 13) may just be discerned in the archway behind the central group of figures.

Teach all Nations

5

When the Second Vatican Council assembled in 1962 there were 3,281 bishops in St Peter's Basilica: the number included 531 from Latin American countries, 296 from Africa and 217 from the United States of America. In the half-century that has since elapsed the decisive shift in the balance of Catholic populations in the world has become even more obvious: the Catholic Church has indeed become universal. There had been loss and gain in the extent of Christendom in the Middle Ages. Some of the eastern churches had been all but overwhelmed by the conquests of Islam, the Latin Kingdom of Jerusalem had been altogether lost, and then, in the Protestant Reformation, at the very birth of the modern world, the north of Europe fell away from Catholic allegiance. What was gained came in the Reconquest of Spain. Yet early in the sixteenth century the newly discovered transatlantic world, and the missionary expansion that it stimulated, inaugurated the greatest age of Catholic advance, on a truly global scale, since the Early Church. Catholicism itself was reinvigorated in the process; its historical development was increasingly defined in relation to the diverse peoples it encountered and to novel problems of institutional organization quite unknown to medieval Christianity.

The expansion showed once again the importance of the religious orders in the evolution of Catholic Christianity. For it was their early enterprise, especially the friars', which had begun to establish an accumulating knowledge of missionary conditions – a consciousness of how subtle were the adjustments that had to be made in representing the Faith within the cultural and social assumptions of peoples untouched by the classical inheritance of the Mediterranean Church. In the east there were still resonances of the first knowledge of Christianity brought to the Indian subcontinent in a tradition that was believed to derive from St Thomas, but it was the mendicant orders of the Middle Ages that began a continuous

Fray Bartolomé de Olmedo accompanied Hernán Cortés during the Conquest of Mexico in 1519–20, and is here shown (by Miguel González, c.1698) exhorting Montezuma II to end human sacrifice and receive Christianity. Behind them severed human limbs are placed in pots. Montezuma suggested an Anglican-style compromise: that the Aztec idols should stand on one side of the temples, facing the Cross and pictures of the Virgin on the other. Cortés rejected the offer.

series of Christian contacts resulting in the planting of Churches which had a direct relationship to Rome. Thus the Franciscans arrived in China with John of Monte Corvino in 1294, and Catholicism reached Indonesia, also at the end of the thirteenth century, when Franciscans travelling to China stopped there on the way; by 1534 they had a mission in the Straits of Malacca. Augustinians had converted the Spanish Philippine islands after their mission arrived in 1565. In the 1580s Franciscans from the Philippines started work in Vietnam, followed almost immediately by Portuguese Dominicans.

The new orders of the Counter Reformation were by then active. The Jesuits organized the Church at Goa in 1542, with the work of St Francis Xavier. In 1582, the Jesuits were active in China, led by Michele Ruggieri and Matteo Ricci. In the west, the Portuguese settlement of Brazil was accompanied by a Jesuit mission from 1549, and the Society entered Spanish America (until then a Franciscan preserve) in 1568. In fact, the Jesuits seemed to turn up everywhere – in Mozambique in the seventeenth century, and even in Ethiopia, that most ancient of Christian societies.

In the New World, the Spanish and the Portuguese Crowns integrated the missions with the colonial administration in a remarkable and systematic structure. It was in order to keep heresy out of the area, and so keep the new countries unitary and homogenous, that the Spanish imposed a *limpieza de sangre* test for European immigrants – a record of three generations of family freedom from heresy. The Franciscans undertook temporal as well as spiritual duties, with the stipends of the friars paid by the government. Soldiers were allocated to their mission stations in order to pacify the Indians. The papacy, and the Council of the Indies, emphatically banned enforced conversions, however, just as the Church had prohibited the compulsory Christianization of Moslems during the Crusades. Doubtless social

RIGHT Church of San Pedro Apóstol, Andahuaylillas, Peru, built early in the 17th century. Churches along the Andean coast of South America learned from the Incas that large stone blocks at the foundation level were good protection against earthquakes; walls of smaller stone or *adobe* rose to tiled roofs in the conventional Spanish manner.

BELOW LEFT In 1769, Fray Junípero Serra, who had come originally from Majorca, was sent by the Spanish Crown to conduct missions in California, travelling as part of Gaspar de Portola's expedition. The journey must have caused Serra great pain, since for most of his life he suffered from incurable leg ulcers. He is remembered still, as one of the founders of modern California.

BELOW RIGHT Most of Serra's Mission Churches still exist, including this one at Carmel. Each station was built a day's journey distant, to facilitate supply and communication. The friars were popular with the converted Indians: when Fray Peyri was recalled to Spain from the Mission San Luis Rey in San Diego, in 1832, thousands followed him to the harbour to bid him farewell.

pressures inclined many Indians to conversion, but the ecclesiastical authorities monitored the observance of correct procedure closely. The settlement of Spanish America was, for a pre-collectivist polity, an extraordinary exercise of state powers. In 1543, the Crown fixed at ten years the time for the friars to complete their work among the Indians in each place, and they were then moved on to the next mission station, and the civil authorities took over. These arrangements, having proved themselves, were confirmed in the Ordinances of 1573. Ten years later, the religious orders were subordinated to episcopal authority in their settlement work, and Catholicism in Spanish America settled down to an impressive stability.

In Portuguese Brazil, the Jesuits, after 1549, continued work initiated by the friars, on very similar lines to the Spanish. Early in the seventeenth century they began to penetrate the vast hinterland from the northern coasts of Pernambuco in the east, and from Quito into the Amazon. Among the last of the great Franciscan missions – and forever remembered in North

America – was the work of Father Junípero Serra, the Evangelist of California. He was born in Majorca in 1713, and emigrated to Mexico in 1749. He was sent by King Carlos III of Spain, in 1769, to establish missions in the military stations set up in California, then part of Spanish America. There were eventually twenty-one missions along the *Camino Real* in California, nine founded by Fray Serra himself before his death in 1784. Most of the Mission churches survive, from San Francisco in the north to San Diego in the south.

The greatest of all the missionaries of this period was St Francis Xavier, an original member of the Society of Jesus with St Ignatius Loyola. He was born in Navarre, a nobleman of Spanish-Basque descent, in 1506. It was while studying in Paris that he took the oath of poverty and service that bound him and the group of friends to the furtherance of Christianity. After Pope Paul III had authorized the Portuguese to employ Jesuits as the evangelists of the east, Xavier undertook his heroic missionary journeys – to the fishermen of the Straits of Malacca, to Sri Lanka, and to Japan (which he reached in 1549). In modern commentary his methods have sometimes been questioned: he has been criticised for insensitivity to oriental religious customs, and has been thought to have relied too closely on the support of the Portuguese colonial authorities. These were not, however, matters that seem to have impeded his success, nor were they uniformly true. Everywhere he went there were conversions, sometimes of enormous numbers. He was also noted for the intensity of his personal spiritual life, and for the memory he left with those who worked with him.

Xavier intended a great work in China, and set out in 1552. He died of fever on the island of Sancian, off the China coast; his body was eventually returned to Goa, where it remains to this day, perfectly preserved and periodically exposed to the faithful, at the basilica of the Bom Jesus. He was canonized in 1622. So great was his respect for all living creatures, and so incorporative was his desire to spread the knowledge of Christ, that he is often depicted iconographically standing by the sea-shore as he preached – even the fish and crabs emerging from the water were attentive to his words. He is remembered in the lovely and sublime sentiments of his hymn, *O Deus, ego amo Te.*

The missionary journeys of the Jesuit St Francis Xavier to the east established a lasting Christian presence which, though usually not numerically great, has proved an essential starting point for the evangelism of subsequent generations. He died in 1552 off the China coast, and his body – miraculously incorrupt – was eventually entombed in the Church of the Bom Jesus (the Good Jesus) in Goa, headquarters of the Jesuits' eastern mission. This wooden statue is in the Bom Jesus and dates from the 17th century.

The late Art Deco (1960) monument to the Portuguese overseas discoveries in Lisbon. The design suggests both a cross and the prow of a ship: religion and trade, Church and State.

That all this missionary energy intensified very early in the sixteenth century indicates several new conditions to which the Catholic Church was sensitive. The long missionary journeys were made possible by the entrepreneurial enterprise of great ports such as Genoa, Palma, Cadiz, Barcelona and Lisbon, and by the improvements in shipping which their merchants financed, usually by versions of joint-stock investment. The invention of the *caravel* enabled an extension of the range of the voyages and increased speed. The discovery of the Americas, and their immediate exploitation by the Iberian Crowns, allowed the Catholic conversion of most of the western hemisphere in an astonishingly short space of time; within a century the Spanish empire even reached into a third of the area now within the United States. From the Spanish colony of Florida, and in Texas and California, Spanish Catholicism began to encounter the Catholic French pushing down the Mississippi valley to Louisiana.

The journeys round the coast of Africa, and to the east, were also the consequence of Iberian sea-power. In each area the material pursuit of wealth by the Spanish and the Portuguese was accompanied by almost visionary anticipations of a providential religious destiny, sometimes expressed with millenarian and apocalyptic speculations. In addition, therefore, to the plundering adventurers and the ruthless merchants, who are now often taken to typify the worldliness of the *Conquistadores,* there were the Catholic idealists, lay and clerical, who regarded the New World as an earthly paradise reserved by God for the creation of a Christian civilization.

These ideas actually originated in Spain itself, in the mystical popular writings produced during the reigns of Ferdinand and Isabella, and suffused, still, with the Catholic zeal generated by the final expulsion of the Moors. The reforms of the Spanish religious orders by Cardinal Cisneros had had the unexpected consequence of preparing them for their great evangelistic work in America and in the Philippines. Events of the Conquest were accorded religious significance. Hernán Cortés was regarded as a new Moses – by Gerónimo de Mendieta, for example, the theoretician of the heightened millennial speculations. Martín Fernández de Enciso compared the Conquest with the entry of the Israelites into the land of Canaan. Columbus himself believed that the Orinoco was one of the four rivers of Eden. (Such images, incidentally, were popularized in a supposedly authoritarian Catholic spiritual culture which Protestant critics were shortly to claim left the faithful ignorant of the Bible.) The foot soldiers of Catholic advance, the friars, were influenced by Joachimite spirituality. Joachim of Fiore, who had died in 1202, had preached a version of apocalyptic mysticism which had degenerated into heretical myths, but was revived and purified in the New World by the Franciscans. A 'Third Age' of mankind was anticipated: a perfected community purged of corrupt institutions and under the patronage of the Spanish Crown and the Catholic Church. This eschatology of colonialism not only cast a new function for Spanish monarchy but also dignified the Indian population – who were to become the human material of the ideal society.

In Brazil, the Portuguese lacked the crusading and mystical psyche of the Spanish: their campaign against the Moors had ended two centuries earlier.

Yet there was a Brazilian millenial vision. It derived from the myth of *Sebastianism*, begun in Portugal in the second half of the sixteenth century, which flowered in the coastal regions of Brazil. There was to be an ideal kingdom, in which the poor would be raised up. Its prophet was the seventeenth-century Jesuit Antonio Vieira. More than the Spanish mysticism, *Sebastianism* had the characteristics of a classic sect, a Church of the disinherited, a mixture of religious egalitarianism and folk spirituality. For the most part, however, Catholic development in the New World was retained within conventional ecclesiastical order.

What is most remarkable about the expansion of Catholicism everywhere in the early modern world is that its dynamism preceded the Reformation. This is an indication of the vitality of the late medieval Church, and a witness to its missionary capabilities on the eve of the great disruption in Europe. The Protestants separated themselves from Rome at just that moment in history when the Catholic Church underwent an expansive renewal. That expansion remained broadly in the control of the papacy, even though for practical reasons the popes had conceded much of the governance of the Church in the New World to the Iberian Crowns. The missionary districts everywhere else were governed by the Sacred Congregation for the Propagation of the Faith in Rome, directed by a Cardinal Prefect. The expertise and bureaucratic efficiency of this body was to be of immense service in the centralization of Roman jurisdiction, and in conditions of very considerable regional diversity. The Sacred Congregation received regular reports from the missionary territories throughout the world and thereby, over the centuries, achieved an unrivalled knowledge of changing affairs. The direct relationship to Rome through the Sacred Congregation operated to preserve new Churches established in sometimes antipathetic political environments, and to enable a long-term view: both England and the United States remained under the formal jurisdiction of Propaganda until 1908. Residence in Rome of priests training for ministry at the various national colleges also assisted uniformity in ecclesiastical strategy.

Despite the medieval conflicts over papal jurisdiction in temporal affairs – which still hung in the atmosphere as a warning of history – the papacy sometimes even took an effective part in legitimizing sovereignty exercised by political rulers in the newly annexed areas of the world. Thus Nicholas V, who became pontiff in 1447, issued a bull which allocated West Africa to the Portuguese. In 1493, Alexander VI divided the world between Spain and Portugal by drawing a line down the globe which passed a hundred leagues to the west of the Cape Verde Islands; Spain got all the land to the west – just then discovered by Columbus. This settlement was adjusted in the Treaty of Tordesillas in 1494, when Spain and Portugal agreed to fix the line at 370 leagues, which, by chance, gave Brazil to Portugal. The New

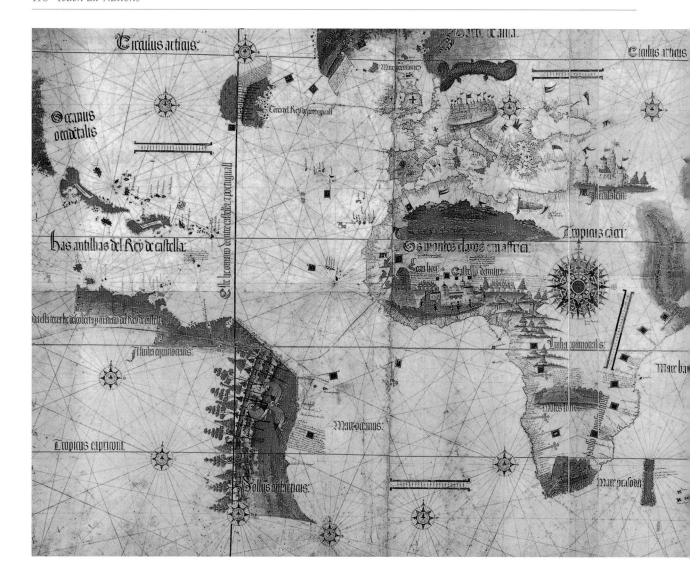

ABOVE 'Cantino' world map, made in Lisbon *c*.1502, showing the demarcation line of the Treaty of Tordesillas through South America. This was the first map to include the discoveries of Columbus. In the Old World, the shape of Africa, after Vasco da Gama, is now virtually complete. Note the prominence of Jerusalem in the centre.

World territories remained firmly under the control of the Iberian Crowns, and so did the Church, but the papacy had shown that it could still deploy its crucial exercise of authority in temporal affairs when called upon to do so.

Many of the issues brought to the Sacred Congregation for the Propagation of the Faith concerned the degree to which Catholicism in the missionary districts could legitimately be expressed in native cultural forms and customs. It was not a new question, and had raised numerous problems both in the ancient world and in the early Christianization of Europe. Most recently, from the perspective of the sixteenth-century missionaries, these problems had occurred in Spain after the Moors, and in the conversion of the pagan peoples of what became Prussia. But conditions in each place varied enormously, and the controversies attached to indigenization of the faith have recurred right up to the present time. They were even evident, in a sophisticated form, in the concepts of 'national' Churches in modern Europe.

The policy of Rome over indigenization was in general flexible but cautious, and judgements were made about the qualities of the cultures the Catholic missionaries were seeking to penetrate – judgements which at times were necessarily relative. There was great reserve in relation to native custom in Latin America and Africa, and an openness to cultural assimilation where, as in the east, learning and civilization had been recognized through episodic contacts for centuries. This distinction – which was never made systematically – indicated another, and related, phenomenon: that Catholicism was astonishingly successful in the conversion of South and Central America yet made so little advance in the east.

The reason is plain. In the west, there was military conquest and the indigenization of European culture could be managed by the governing elites; there it was possible for the religious concepts and customs of the conquered to survive as sub-cultures. In the east, the Catholic missionaries were impressed by the sophistication of the cultures they encountered, but indigenization could do no more than scratch the surface. St Francis Xavier himself admired Japanese culture. In the west, native customs did not appear admirable, and the Indians' religious practices were absorbed by a series of local syncretisms: the Indians seem to have accepted Christianity with enthusiasm, and its representations in familiar cultural forms was encouraged by Church policy as a conscious exercise of indigenization. Thus surviving Mexican customs were not a hidden adhesion to pagan ways, an implicit protest against Christianization, but considered responses to missionary strategy.

The Church itself was not dismissive of indigenous religious ideas. Studies of customs and beliefs were made by the friars, and one of these, the

RIGHT It was the policy of the Catholic Church to indigenize the faith by representing it in the styles and symbols of the cultures being addressed by missioners. This seems to have been official strategy from the earliest expansions of the Church. This is the Jesuit Church of the Assumption (Namban-dera) in Japan; by Kano Soshu, 16th century. It has the distinctive appearance of a Japanese shrine of the period.

Historia Natural y Moral de las Indias, by the Jesuit priest José de Acosta, published in 1590, became a classic work of reference. Because there was an appreciation that Indian religion was unlike European, the indigenous peoples were exempted from the jurisdiction of the Inquisition, and because of explicit papal teaching about their natural rights, in Paul III's bull of 1537, *Sublimis Deus*, they were protected in their freedom and property and were not to be depressed into slavery. At the University of Salamanca in Spain Francisco de Vitoria expounded the principle that all native peoples had rights, even if not converted to Christianity, and that native customs were not to be regarded as inferior. There were, of course, exceptions to this teaching, when local practices seemed incompatible with natural law as expounded in Thomism and Roman law.

In the modern world it has become usual for much Christian missionary work of the past to be judged culturally insensitive or downright oppressive – as if the zeal of the missionaries was exercised without any kind of responsiveness to the beliefs of the people among whom they laboured. Modern opinion, however, is often based upon appreciation of the art and social organization of the peoples who came into contact with Europeans, disregarding their morals or the effects of their religious practices. It was the missionaries who ended mass human sacrifice in Central America in the sixteenth century, who secured the abolition of *suttee* rites in India in 1829, who were martyred in Uganda in 1884 when they attempted to outlaw systematic pederasty at the court of the King of Buganda, and who everywhere used their influence to halt inter-tribal genocide. Would modern people have acted any differently?

Sometimes there appeared to be no real possibility of indigenization. In 1846, for example, Spanish monks began work in Western Australia, but achieved little: aboriginal religious consciousness derived from quasi-mystical attachment to land and to tribal arrangements that were evidently impossible to express in the Catholic concepts of sin and redemption. The conversion of the aboriginals only proved effective after the later disintegration of their culture and their drift to the cities. The Araucanian Indians of Chile were also resistant to conversion, or to pacification, after three centuries of attempts by the friars. Charles Darwin was to observe, in the 1860s, that they were too low in what he considered the scale of human life to be capable of civilization.

The rise and respectability of racist categorization in nineteenth-century western thought and anthropology, indeed, were in contrast to the pragmatism of the earlier missionaries of the Catholic Church, and to the belief, to which they adhered, that every soul could receive the divine grace necessary for salvation. Nineteenth-century missionaries, while not despairing in their efforts, sometimes recognized an uphill journey – though one occasionally

Modern mission schools continue to associate the Catholic faith with general education and the acquisition of skills. These aborigine girls attend classes with a nun at a mission in Arnhem Land, Northern Territory, Australia.

directed by faulty social observation. In his book *The Catholic Church and the Kaffir*, published in 1880, Bishop James Ricards, Vicar Apostolic of the Eastern District in the Cape Province of South Africa, offered an analysis that inclined him to suppose the Bantu incapable of religious thought.

In Japan, by contrast, it appeared that assimilation of Catholicism, in one instance, anyway, was astonishingly durable. After the most fearful persecution, in 1640 the Catholic missionaries, and all other foreigners, were expelled from Japan. They did not return until a treaty with the French in 1859. In that year the missionaries who re-entered the country were amazed to discover thousands of Catholics in small local communities. Without a regular priesthood, and no access to Catholic education, or external contacts, they had preserved their faith for two centuries.

In many places the Catholic missions sought to protect indigenous peoples, and sometimes their culture, from the disrupting effects of uncontrolled European exploitation. The most well-known example is the *Reductiones* conducted by the Jesuits in Paraguay. These communities, on reservations of land given by King Philip III of Spain, comprised some hundred thousand Guaraní Indians, in thirty settlements, by the end of the seventeenth century. A strictly paternalistic regime was governed by the Jesuits. Land was held in common; there was no money; white people were excluded; each colony had a church, a school and model housing. This description makes them sound like an anticipation of the ideal socialist communitarianism of nineteenth-century social experimentation in, for example, the North American frontier, but the intention of the Jesuits' *Reductiones* in Paraguay was practical. The produce was marketed

ABOVE The Jesuit mission in Japan, planted by St Francis Xavier, incurred political disfavour towards the end of the 16th century, when the conversions were interrupted as corrupting national culture. In 1622, fifty-one Christians, both native and foreign, were executed in Nagasaki, depicted here in a wall-painting in the Gesù in Rome.

on capitalist lines, and the purpose was ethnic protection. These were not attempts to build ideal societies, nor was the culture of the Guaraní especially highly regarded in them: the reserves existed to protect them. When the Jesuits were expelled from their territories by Spain in 1767, and by Portugal and France in the same year, the *Reductiones* declined sharply, and despite efforts by colonial officials to keep them in operation, the Indians deserted to the towns and to the forests, and after thirty years the Guaraní colonies were in ruins.

A comparable social experiment begun in Mexico in the sixteenth century by Vasco de Quiroga, later Bishop of Michoácan, by gathering the Indians into collective farms, also proved ephemeral. In nineteenth-century South Africa some Trappist monks from Germany sought to protect the blacks from white settler exploitation, and from the destructive effects of contact with white culture. In 1882, they set up a model community in Natal, under the leadership of Prior Franz Pfanner. Zulus were gathered at Mariannhill, where a church, a school and model housing were constructed. A second community was started in 1886 at Reichenau, and then a few others. By the end of the century there were twenty-eight. The ideological purpose was very explicit and accomplished with Germanic precision. Prior Pfanner was seeking to restore the ideal relationships of the medieval Catholic world, as understood by nineteenth-century romanticism, with guilds and common labour beneath the canopy of Catholic order. Protestant experiments, pioneered by the Moravians, also arranged race segregation in ideal communities as a solution to the disintegrating consequences for tribal life of white contact in South Africa.

The kinds of social problem, of which these schemes were attempted palliatives, also made difficulties for officials in Rome when it came to arranging for indigenous priests to serve in the young Churches. The Council of Trent, in its provisions intended to achieve high educational standards for the priesthood, was extremely difficult to apply in the mission districts. There was, again, a difference between Latin America, with its teeming populations of converted Indians, and the eastern hemisphere, with its educated and culturally superior elites.

In 1576 Pope Gregory XIII instructed the missionaries to learn the Indian languages with greater application, lamenting the need, then being experienced, of having to ordain *mestizos* who were below Tridentine educational standards. Raising full-blooded Indians to the priesthood was already banned on practical grounds – again of educational levels. Considerations of race, as such, were not regarded as proper: this was seen in the veneration of St Martín de Porres, a mulatto born in Lima in 1589, who entered the Dominican order and served the poor of the city until his death in 1639. He has remained a subject of popular devotion in the Catholic world.

A number of colleges to educate the sons of Indian chiefs were opened in the sixteenth and seventeenth centuries, but were unsuccessful in attracting recruits. Priests in Latin America remained Spanish or Portuguese until the end of the eighteenth century. Even in the Philippines, where the Spanish had established the only really sizeable Catholic Church in the east, the ministry was largely composed of members of religious orders sent from Spanish Mexico – Augustinians in particular. The episcopal see of Manila was founded in 1579, but the first Filipino bishop was not appointed until 1905. Early in the twentieth century both Benedict XV and Pius XI declared the importance of an indigenous priesthood.

In the eastern missions native converts were admitted to the ministry early: in Japan in 1601, in Vietnam in 1668, in China a converted peasant was made Vicar Apostolic of the Northern District in 1674. In 1637, a Brahmin from Goa was appointed Vicar Apostolic for the non-Portuguese parts of India. In the nineteenth century, however, the issue of caste – so sensitive within Indian society itself – raised formidable difficulties over the ordination of indigenous clergy. Rome gave permission for lower castes to become priests in 1836; but in 1855 the Bishop of Coimbatore felt obliged to resign his see because of his reluctance to train indigenous clergy. In so many areas of Indian public life caste continued, as it still does, to complicate religious policy.

In the African countries, by contrast, ordinations of indigenous converts came rapidly. This was the more remarkable since the evangelization of the hinterland occurred at the height of a period, in the later nineteenth century, when European thought was particularly susceptible to categorizing native peoples according to stereotypes intended to identify them upon scales of supposed cultural maturity. In Uganda, nevertheless, the first African Catholic priests were ordained in 1913, and the first African bishop, Joseph Kiwanuka, was consecrated in 1939 – the first Black African Catholic bishop in modern times.

Before the rise of Ultramontanism in the nineteenth century, with its exclusivist insistence on the replication of the styles of Italianate religious practice everywhere, there was considerable pragmatism in the Church's attitude to issues of cultural adaptation and indigenization. Sometimes this expressed itself in small but telling gestures. St Francis Xavier himself dressed in the clothes of a Japanese priest in the two years he lived in the country after 1549. Both Michele Ruggieri and Matteo Ricci, who led the Jesuit mission in China after 1582, retained the ceremonies and often the vocabulary of Chinese traditional religion. Ricci wore Chinese dress, and himself observed the ritualized customs of ancestor-worship. Roberto de Nobili, preacher of the Gospel in Madurai until his death in 1656, lived the life of an Indian *guru*, and succeeded in making high-caste conversions. His methods, however, were criticised by officials in Rome, and there were comparable misgivings about the adaptation of rites and liturgical forms elsewhere. Often complaints were aggravated by domestic antipathy towards the Jesuits, who were proving themselves the most inventive and adaptable in the presentation of the Faith – largely, perhaps, because their superior education prepared them for an enhanced appreciation of overseas cultures.

P. MATTHÆVS RICCIVS MACERAT.
of the Society of Iesus. the first propagator
of the Christian Religion in the Single of China.

LY PAVLVS GREAT COLAVS OI
the Chinese propagator of Christian Law.

Jesuit priests in China in the dress of Chinese traditional religion. On the left is Matteo Ricci, who entered the country in 1582 and remained for seventeen years.

In the seventeenth century the Jesuit missions in India were especially adept at incorporating social customs: Brahmins were divided from other castes in church by partitioned areas. Pope Clement XI was sufficiently uneasy about Jesuit flexibility for him to instigate enquiries into the Malabar rite encouraged by Nobili in India – a liturgical use believed to derive from the Malabar Christians who had been in India since the fourth century. Caution from the curial officials usually prevailed. In 1742 two bulls of Benedict XIV prohibited the Chinese rites. It was a policy not reversed until 1939.

In Latin America, the interpretation of indigenization was paradoxically reversed late in the nineteenth century, when first liberal and then Marxist secular intellectuals and politicians attempted to undermine the influence of Catholicism in society. They saw it as an impediment to social progress. Armed with anthropological orthodoxy, and with an eager propensity to represent the Indian peasantry as a rural proletariat straining to overthrow the Hispanic landowning class, the critics of the Church sought to revive public consciousness of an imagined harmonious pre-Conquest social order. This was, in fact, a kind of secular counterpart to the Catholic vision, current at the time and dependent no less upon social romanticism, of an ideal medieval world in which there was also harmony. With an acute knowledge of some of the less felicitous aspects of pre-Conquest society however – the human sacrifice and systematic genocide – the Catholic Church was not surprisingly unhappy about the secularists' propaganda.

The new myths about pre-Conquest society were most lucidly formulated by the Aprista *pensadores* of Peru, early in the twentieth century, and by José Carlos Mariátegui – who insisted that Catholicism was nothing more than the spiritual arm of the white exploitation that destroyed Indian cultures. It was in some measure as a reaction to the *indigenismo* intellectuals that Latin American Catholic thinkers of the 1920s and 1930s were attracted to Hispanic Fascism: it appeared to be an opponent of the cultural relativism of the Marxist promoters of *indigenismo* idealism.

LEFT The Philippines – now one of the most Catholic areas in the world – was originally evangelized largely by Augustinians from Mexico. Here is the Church of San Agustín in Manila, completed in 1606. The influence of the Chinese labourers who built the church is evident in the stone Chinese lions along the base of the walls: a reminder of the lions that protect temples in the Chinese traditional religion.

ABOVE St Paul's Church, Macao, China. Detail of the façade showing the congruence of western and eastern artistic decorative styles. Dragons resemble those that guard the entrances of Chinese temples, and there are Buddhist flying figures (*apsaras*). Explanatory texts are in Chinese characters – the first in any Christian building. The indigenization was part of the original intention of the Jesuit designers, Carlo Spinola and Giovanni Niccolò, in 1601.

The reality, in fact, was that Catholicism in Latin America had from the very beginning been penetrated by indigenous cultural and social practices in the rural areas, where most of the Indians lived. These penetrations went some way beyond the artistic decorative devices used in church buildings by native labourers and which were a feature everywhere. In the eastern hemisphere Chinese craftsmen employed the symbols of their own traditional religion in the decoration of Catholic buildings. Thus the Church of San Agustín in Manila, begun in 1599, has stone lions along its façade, just as Chinese temples do. And at the seventeenth-century Church of San Paulo in Portuguese Macau there are dragons incised on the stonework.

Latin America, however, produced the phenomenon of 'idols under the altar'. Native Indian customs reasserted themselves in the worship of the Christianized populations and in their sense of the numinous encountered

ABOVE The silver and gold of the New World were used in the exuberant decoration of the Baroque churches of Mexico, and the Indian craftsmen often represented angels and *putti* as having Indian features. This is the church of San Francisco Acatepec, built around 1730.

in everyday life. The sublime Baroque churches put up by the Spanish and Portuguese colonialists were filled with statues and painted plaster mouldings in which the native craftsmen represented the Catholic saints, and the Blessed Virgin, as Indians like themselves, with sad eyes and impassive expressions, suffering for the Faith. The Saviour himself is shown, in a thousand tableaux, as a bowed figure, bleeding on his way to Calvary as he carries his cross: here were all the privations of a defeated people, offered up in unconscious folk-art depictions of the adversities of life.

The intensity of Indian devotional practices heightened the scorn of the twentieth-century secularists, and accounts for the desecration of churches in Mexico by General Pancho Villa in 1913, and the abuse of the Reserved Sacrament by Federal soldiers fighting the *Cristeros* in the Mexican popular uprising of 1927. At Puebla, in Mexico, the convent of Santa Monica

ABOVE LEFT San Isidro Labrador, patron of agricultural labourers and a popular figure, therefore, among the *campesinos* of Latin America. Effigies like this, with cactus-weave hat and woollen *serape*, are still made to carry in the processions of thanksgiving for the harvest.

ABOVE RIGHT St Mary of the Angels; a procession to celebrate the feast of the Assumption in Guatemala. Devotions to the Virgin were always inseparable from Catholic life, but were particularly encouraged by the spread of Ultramontane devotional styles in the 19th century. Many areas have local cults of particular representations or attributes of the Virgin.

managed to survive the general dissolution of religious institutions during the hostile administration of Calles in the 1920s and Cárdenas in the 1930s; the nuns retreated to hidden rooms where they existed, unknown to the world for many years, secretly protected by neighbouring sympathizers. In 1934, they were discovered and expelled. Freemasons then turned their convent into a museum of atheism, similar to those in the contemporaneous Soviet Union. Graham Green described the lives of the nuns of Santa Monica in his book *The Lawless Roads*, after visiting the museum in 1939.

Indigenization of the Catholic Faith was an important issue in each era of Catholic evangelization. And it remains important, as one of the main themes in modern evaluation of missionary strategy in both Catholic and Protestant thinking. At the very beginning of the advance in Latin America the Church was conscious of it. There was a sense in which they had no choice, for the tenacity of Indian practices also presented itself from the beginning. The great sign of this was the apparition of the Virgin herself, in the form of an Indian princess, at Tepeyac Hill to the north of Mexico City in 1531. The site had been venerated by the Aztecs and was a place of fertility rites. The Virgin appeared to Juan Diego, a converted Indian: she told him to gather roses from among the rocks of the hillside and to carry them in his *serape* (cloak) to the Bishop of Mexico. When he followed her instructions, and opened the *serape* to present the flowers to the Bishop, her features were found to have been miraculously impressed, within a sunburst nimbus, upon the cactus fibres.

The *serape* may still be seen, with its image of the Virgin of Guadalupe, in the basilica at Mexico City – her serene features virtually indistinguishable from those of the thousands of modern Indians who come to pray at the shrine each day. The banners of Guadalupe were carried by the *Cristeros* in 1927; she has been proclaimed by the papacy as the Patroness of Latin America. On a visit to the shrine in 1979 John Paul II placed the people of Mexico under her special protection. It is a curious twist of fate – or sign of providence – that the *Religiosidad Popular* which early twentieth-century social progressives regarded as so baneful and

superstitious, as a hindrance to the advancement of the poor, should later in the century have become, for a generation of Catholic radicals, an indication of authentic proletarian virtue.

A new intellectual vogue for folk spirituality fell upon the world in the 1960s; it was a dimension of wider attempts to represent Catholic teachings as compatible with Marxist social analysis. At the Second General Conference of Latin American Bishops, held at Medellín, in Colombia, in 1968, further study of *Religiosidad Popular* was encouraged – indeed a resolution suggested it should not be understood in bourgeois intellectual categories but should be recognized as the authentic product of working-class consciousness. Indigenization was once again officially sanctioned. There was, however, a difference. In the previous centuries indigenization in Latin America had in reality been on terms set by the peasantry; it was they who expected religion to be indifferent to change, not the priests, and whose insistence on preserving the magic of their ancient folk beliefs should simply be carried on within the practice of Catholicism. In the 1960s, it was the intellectuals who wanted the old ways to be perpetuated, it was they who reinterpreted the peasants' faithfulness to tradition as

The most potent symbol of the indigenization of the faith in the Americas was the appearance of the Virgin, in the likeness of a native Indian princess, on a rocky hillside just outside Mexico City in 1531 – a decade after the Conquest. The Virgin of Guadalupe was named by Leo XIII as 'Queen of Mexico and Empress of the Americas' in 1895, and Juan Diego, to whom she delivered her message, was canonized by John Paul II in 2002. She has become a powerful symbol of Latin American identity; the *serape* in the basilica at Mexico City depicts her gentle features in a sunburst nimbus as she inclines towards her followers in the New World.

social protest, backed up by Marxist analysis – and as good art as well. The only difference really was that the Aprista writers had been secularist atheists whereas the 1960s enthusiasts for *Religiosidad Popular* were radicalized Catholic priests.

After the heroic age, the extra-European expansion of the Catholic Church continued to encounter the same difficulties and successes, but also some new and very different ones. The institutions of modern society and government changed the patterns of development decisively. In Latin America and in the Philippines the Church had been nurtured under the direct control of the Iberian crowns; that ceased with the independence movements early in the nineteenth century, with the birth of the new republics – and in the Philippines when the islands passed from the control of Spain to the United States in 1898.

In Africa, the European colonial administrations secured state structures with which the Catholic missionaries were broadly familiar, since they often came from the social classes and the same nations as the ruling white elites. The difficulties of indigenizing the Faith showed some major shifts, because of the very different types of social organization the Church sought to penetrate. Improved communications in the nineteenth century, the sophistication of the expert knowledge available through the personnel and archives of the Sacred Congregation for the Propagation of the Faith, and enhanced enlightenment in the methods of colonial administration by the European governments, meant that Catholic expansion in Africa was rapid.

The White Fathers have conducted missions in many parts of central and eastern Africa since the middle of the 19th century.

The Society of African Missions, founded by Melchior de Marion Brésillac in 1856, and continued after his death in Sierra Leone, from fever, in 1859, by Augustine Planque, set a model which was widely followed. Planque was confirmed as Superior-General of the Society by Pius IX, and work then began in Nigeria, down the West African coast, and in Egypt. The Sisters of St Joseph of Cluny, established in 1807, had also worked in Sierra Leone. In South Africa, the Catholic Church was separated from the Vicariate of Mauritius in 1827, when Bishop Patrick Griffiths was appointed by Rome as Vicar Apostolic of Cape Province. In Uganda, the White Fathers arrived in 1879. They experienced, however, a high level of denominational rivalry with Protestants – a measure of discord amply exploited by the Bugandan monarchy. In Africa, as elsewhere in missionary work, it was the religious orders who were leaders in evangelization. In the Portuguese territory of Angola the Capuchins had been making impressive numbers of conversions since the second half of the seventeenth century; in Mozambique the Jesuits had secured the establishment of a Vicariate even earlier, in 1612.

The Christian presence created as a result of early missionary enterprise was placed on a regular basis of ecclesiastical jurisdiction by Rome as soon as conditions allowed in each area. Those conditions were necessarily more easily reached in African colonial countries, which were governed according to sympathetic political regimes, than in some of the missions that had existed far longer but operated under powers which might be less amenable. Sometimes the missions had to be reconstituted several times. Thus in Japan the modern Catholic Church really dates, as an independent jurisdiction, from the Vicariate established in 1868 and the full hierarchy set up in 1891. The first indigenous bishop, named by the Vatican in 1927, was Januarius Mayusaki of Nagasaki.

China had a very disturbed modern Catholic history. Many of the faithful were killed in the Boxer Rising of 1900; many were killed or dispersed during the Communist Revolution in 1949 and in the Cultural Revolution of 1966. In 1926, the papacy had authorized the consecration of six Chinese

The Cathedral of Guangzhou (Canton) in 1959. The original Gothic magnificence is set against the municipal collection point outside; during the Cultural Revolution the building was requisitioned for use as a carpet warehouse.

bishops, but hostility between the plainly healthy Church and the Communist state in the 1950s led to a sharp deterioration of relations between the government and the Vatican, and to the state's attempt to set up an independent 'national' Church. India, in contrast, despite some recent clashes between Hindu nationalism and Christian educational institutions, has shown a stable modern development. The first Indian Cardinal was created in 1952; there are now around sixteen million Catholics. In Pakistan, a hierarchy was set up by the Vatican in 1950.

The Catholic Churches of the nations that were once dominions of the British Empire have developed in relatively peaceful conditions. British colonial policy towards the Catholics – in some contrast to the remnants of the penal laws still on the statute book in Britain itself at the start of the nineteenth century – was generally supportive. This was usually for pragmatic reasons: the avoidance of controversy, the securing of allegiance. In Britain

OPPOSITE This photograph, taken in 1954, shows seminarists at St Joseph's Apostolic Seminary at Trivandrum in South India. Here all is traditional Catholicism – including the splendid Gothic chapel.

RIGHT St Patrick's College, Maynooth, Co. Kildare, Ireland. This is the greatest of the Irish seminaries for the training of priests, not only for service in Ireland and America but throughout the world mission field. The college was established in 1795 with an annual grant from the British government, in the hope that Irish seminarists would no longer resort to France for training – and possibly become acquainted with revolutionary ideas. This is the Chapel, by J.J. McCarthy, 1890.

JOANNES CARROLL, S.T.D. ⟂ JOHN CARROLL, D.D.

John Carroll, appointed Bishop of Baltimore in November 1789, and consecrated nine months later, was the first Catholic bishop in the United States. In 1808, he became Archbishop, with four new dioceses administered by suffragens. He inspired the founding of many Catholic educational and charitable institutions.

itself the state paid for the education of Catholic priests at Maynooth in Ireland from the end of the eighteenth century, passed the Catholic Emancipation Act in 1829, and subsidized Catholic schools from the mid-nineteenth century. In 1869, parliament legislated to Disestablish the Irish Protestant Church – a direct concession to Irish Catholic sentiment and its cultural association with nationalist politics. Ireland remained one of the most Catholic countries in the world until it began a practical process of secularization in the 1970s.

In Quebec, the French had arrived in 1605. The customary Catholic rights and property were secured by law in 1774 after the British conquest. A simple oath of allegiance to the crown was allowed without the requirement, which existed in the United Kingdom, to subscribe the Royal Supremacy in religion. In 1844, Quebec became a metropolitan see. A Jesuit became the first Catholic bishop in the United States. John Carroll, from an old Catholic Maryland family, was consecrated in England in 1790 as the Bishop of Baltimore. In 1808, his diocese became a metropolitan see. The constitutional separation of Church and State in America spared the Catholics from interference in the internal jurisdiction of the Church, but it also meant that the Church could not benefit, as it did elsewhere in the English-speaking world, from state financial assistance with its institutions. A Benedictine monk, J.B. Polding, became the first Catholic bishop in Australia in 1835, and in 1848 the first two Catholic dioceses were established in New Zealand. The first Maori bishop was appointed by the Vatican in 1988.

Early Jesuit missions to the Huron
Indians of New France (Quebec)
encountered vigorous opposition
in the years 1634–50, which
resulted in several martyrdoms.

The great institutional gain in this enormous expansion of the Church was by the papacy – saved from being marginalized in Europe as a result of the growth first of nationalism and then of the collectivist modern state; a victim of the seeping secularization of social custom and of the descent of the populations into individualism in religion. The expansion, precisely because Church and State have in most places been separated in modern times, allowed Rome exclusive control of the growing extra-European Churches. The result has been a uniform and centralized institution, truly universal in vision, challenged, often, because of that very independence, but unrivalled nevertheless. The loss of the States of the Church in Italy coincided historically with the addition of huge numbers of new Churches set in wider dimensions. The one thing the papacy could never have predicted – the success of voluntarism in religion, of a vigorous Church without the political support of the state – turned out to be of enormous benefit. The papacy now has a universal role in a sense it never had before. The Pope is widely recognized as the most important religious leader in the world, and receives the respect he never enjoyed when he was an Italian sovereign, a ruler among the competing rulers of Europe.

CHARITAS DEI
DIFFVSA EST IN CORDIBVS NOSTRIS Rom. 5

S. IN NO: CEN: TIVS

S. ZOZI: MVS.

S. CÆLE: STI: NVS.

S. BONI: FA: CIVS.

PELAGIVS.

CÆLESTIVS. IVLIANVS.

CORNELII IANSENII
EPISCOPI IPRENSIS
ET
IN ACADEMIA LOVANIENSI QVONDAM
S. TH: DOCT: ET PROFESSORIS REGII
AVGVSTINVS

LOVANII
TYPIS ET SVMPTIBVS
IACOBI ZEGERI.

Cum Gratia & priuilegio S. Cæsareæ & Catholicæ Maiestatis. An: 1640.

6

The Church and the Modern State

Cornelius Jansen, Bishop of Ypres after 1636, wrote the *Augustinus* between 1628 and 1638. The work was published after his death in 1640. It interpreted St Augustine's writings in a manner familiar from Calvinist texts produced during the Protestant Reformation, especially in emphasizing the significance of Justification by faith alone. Jansenism attracted Catholic reformist groups of many sorts and came to express the dissidence of those opposed to papal centralization in the Church. The title page of *Augustinus* shows various popes being inspired by St Augustine's exegesis.

The triumphalist atmosphere of the Counter Reformation, and the successful extension of Catholicism in the overseas world, did not prepare the Church for the disruptions it afterwards encountered within the Catholic nations of Europe itself. Protestantism had defined itself within those north European states whose princes had sponsored it largely as a dimension of their secular ambitions; yet the religious map still seemed uncertain. No one could foresee that the division of Christendom into rival camps was to prove permanent. The preceding separation, between Orthodoxy and Catholicism, rather slipped from memory as the eastern Church disappeared from sight after the conquest of Constantinople by the Turks in 1453. The pope had become the only Christian leader who was still sustained by an international bloc of nations. What could not be predicted, however, was that the west European Catholic powers would themselves fall out with the papacy over the principles that were to govern the relations of Church and State. The issues raised, in the eighteenth and nineteenth centuries, in effect involved a resumption of those that had produced the Reformation upheaval in the sixteenth. The success of Protestantism then had resulted from the beginnings of the modern state, and national definitions of sovereignty. The kings who had sponsored the Protestant reformers used the religious issues they pushed to the forefront of debate as the occasion to assert their authority over the only institutions in their realms that owed an external allegiance, to the papacy. The Church also had, in a pre-collectivist world, monopoly of the educational and charitable institutions in their nations, as well as a significant stake in economic activity and landholding. The Reformation represented the consolidation of the kings' sovereignty: they nationalized the Church.

It had seemed as if the successful reform and reorganization of Catholicism, in the same years, had drawn a line beneath the changes. But the remaining Catholic nations – Spain, Portugal, France, Bavaria, and the Italian states – had, as it turned out, experienced the same national impulsions that had motivated the Protestant ones, and they, too, insisted on claiming rights over the Church appropriate to what were perceived to be the realities of modern statecraft. The result was three centuries of periodic tension between Rome and the Catholic powers. By the nineteenth century the addition of liberal ideology, especially within the literate middle classes, and the related diffusion within the intelligentsia of the secular ideals of the eighteenth-century *Philosophes*, produced an insistence on the policy of separating Church and State which the Catholic sovereigns in general resisted but which they also exploited in order to secure increased control of the Catholic institutions in their countries. Within the new terms of reference a greater degree of separation between Church and State tended to mean the subordination of the Church to the State. Resulting upheavals took the form of contests in each nation about the rights and privileges of the Catholic Church, and the degree to which papal authority ought to be circumscribed. The rhetoric had changed, but the papacy found itself back in the world of the medieval Investiture Controversy, compounded by the rise of a body of secular opinion, and complicated by the increased range of powers available to modern sovereign states.

Cornelius Jansen, the Bishop of Ypres, is said to have read each of the works of St Augustine ten times, presumably in order to secure an adequate grasp of their meaning. His resulting exposition, *Augustinus*, was published in 1640 – two years after his death. It interpreted the doctrine of grace, of Justification by faith only, in a manner that had a clear affinity to the Protestant polemics of the Reformation, and was accordingly condemned in a bull of 1653, *Cum Occasione*. Jansenist ideas had the misfortune of incurring the plentiful disapproval of the Jesuits; Jansen had brought this upon himself by opposing the canonizations both of Ignatius Loyola

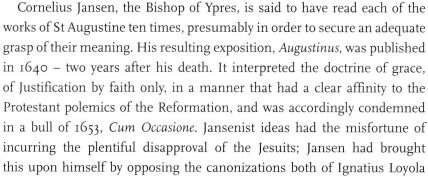

and of Francis Xavier, the two leading Jesuits of the Counter Reformation Catholic expansion. Anti-Jesuit sentiment in the Catholic Church generally, however, and especially among the Franciscans and the Dominicans, somewhat assisted receptivity to Jansenist ideas. Hence the growth of Jansenism among the clergy in a manner distinctly reminiscent of Luther's cult within early Protestantism.

Jansenism was broadcast by Saint-Cyran, Jansen's collaborator and publicist. The movement of opinion strengthened and

In 1713, Jansenism, by then widely distributed throughout western Europe, was condemned in the bull *Unigenitus Dei Filius*. An 18th-century engraving shows Christ himself, surrounded by Jansenists, rejecting the bull. It was not Jansen's understanding of the doctrine of Justification itself that alarmed Catholic authorities so much as the influence of his legacy in providing a vehicle for local reinterpretations of the Faith.

A French calendar of 1686 exhibits approval of Louis XIV's Revocation of the Edict of Nantes in the preceding year. The earlier toleration of the Huguenot Protestants had come to be seen as destructive of French national unity.

persisted. It was again condemned, in the bull *Unigenitus* of 1713. By then it had moved out of the Low Countries and France, where it became mixed with Gallicanism, and penetrated the clergy of Austria and the Grand Duchy of Tuscany. Jansenism was by then being interpreted as support for the authority of the bishops against papal universalist sovereignty over the Church, and so became, to that extent, a rebirth of conciliarist ideas. In France, some Jansenists also sought to diminish royal authority over the Church. There was much idealistic writing about the nature of priesthood in the Early Church, and its supposed freedom from hierarchy. Jansenism, in effect, was a resuscitation of Reformation controversy, also led by the clergy, and also having the potential for monarchical sponsorship as a means of securing national regulation of Catholicism.

Gallicanism was also a new version of an older threat to the universality of the Church. Catholic sovereigns had always made claims about episcopal appointments and about the disposal of ecclesiastical property. These, however, had in the Middle Ages been promoted in the limited context of a feudalized Church operating in a feudal society of highly localized obligations and loyalties. That had elicited tensions enough; in the new world of modern concepts of national sovereignty they were considerably enlarged. Louis XIV issued the Gallican Articles in 1682. They asserted the independence of the French Crown in the temporalities of ecclesiastical administration. They also – and this referred back to preceding areas of past conflict – claimed that the powers of a general council were superior to those of the pope. The French clergy were required to assent to the Articles. Innocent XI refused to invest episcopal nominees presented by the French king.

Yet the attrition of Church and State was not allowed to proceed to division by either party: the papacy had an established preparedness to allow the Catholic sovereigns a measure of control over the Church, and the French monarchy was becoming wary of the progress of Jansenism among the clergy, and revoked the Edict of Nantes, the toleration of the Huguenot Protestants, in 1685. The French king was not prepared to assert his sovereignty, that is to say, by backing the Jansenists the way the German princes had backed the Lutherans in the sixteenth century. The Gallican Articles remained part of the French constitution, and formed the basis of the Concordat of 1801.

Jansenism was the inspiration of the most significant intellectual assault from within the Church itself upon papal claims made in the eighteenth century: the *De Statu Ecclesiae* of Fabronius (Bishop Nikolaus von Hontheim), published in 1763. He was professor of Roman law in the University of Trier; his intention was to reconcile Protestants to the Church by removing those papal teachings to which they most objected – papal universal authority and the superiority of the pope over general councils. Like Acton a century later, he contended, with relish, that papal claims did not stand up to historical verification.

The ideas and actual policies of the Jansenists did not amount to a coherent movement, as such, but they generated an extremely pervasive atmosphere in which papal concepts of the Church were scrutinized and sometimes discarded. And it spread most dangerously, from the perspective of Rome, to the territories of the Holy Roman Emperor. Maria Theresa, as Empress of Austria, a loyal Catholic, had assented to the withdrawal of tax exemption from the clergy, to monastic regulation by the state, to the abolition of rights of sanctuary, and to the removal of many saints' days from the calendar. This set a kind of norm in the tariff of royal control over the Church in the age of Enlightenment.

Joseph II, as Holy Roman Emperor between 1765 and 1790, extended it: there was a Toleration Edict in 1781; crown permission was required for the receipt of papal documents; papal authority over Austrian subjects was reduced to what were considered 'spiritualities' by the government. The entire Catholic Church was reorganized within Austria, both the dioceses and the parochial boundaries. Monastic property was seized by the state. The public was forbidden to kneel before the Sacred Host when carried in procession, or to kiss relics. The contemplative religious orders were dissolved and four hundred houses were closed: they failed the test of utility. It was the regular clergy who performed educational and charitable works who were spared, stripped of some of their property. The reforms, furthermore, were unpopular – the people preferred the old ways, before the agents of the Enlightenment introduced the tyranny of reason to their observances.

There were echoes here, again, of the Protestant Reformation; a re-enactment of the methods of Henry VIII in England, whose policies were, in fact, actually in the minds of the eighteenth-century Catholic sovereigns and their advisers. No wonder Rome was alarmed. Pius VI visited Joseph II in Vienna to spell out the irregularities inherent in his actions. But they were not abandoned. Indeed, they were replicated in Tuscany in 1786, where the Grand Duke Leopold was Joseph II's brother, and they were distributed to those parts of Italy, adjacent to the States of the Church, where Austria was for dynastic reasons influential: to Piedmont, Naples and Parma. It seemed as if the Catholic countries were carving out a new reformation without formally breaking with Rome. For the papacy, a period of extreme danger to the integrity of the Faith seemed imminent. It came, together with the fulfilment of Rome's worst fears, in France.

The Revolution of 1789 unleashed the power of the state over religious institutions with apocalyptic decisiveness. Throughout much of Europe it led to the almost complete collapse of the organization of the Catholic Church, to the actual removal of the Pope from Rome, to the triumph of radical Deism, and sometimes even of official atheism. It led also to the eventual restoration of a pre-revolutionary order in which Rome, fearful of a repetition, embraced legitimist monarchy, formerly its foe, as the very guarantee of its existence – and thereby placed itself in opposition to the liberal ideas that came to govern nineteenth-century social and political progress.

What was most shocking about the events of the Revolution, in the view of the papacy, was not the killing of bishops and priests (some thousands

The collapse of the French monarchy in August 1792 meant the Catholic Church lost one of its last remaining constitutional safeguards. Attacks upon the clergy increased. This engraving by Charles Maurand shows the massacre of priests in September 1792.

were murdered), nor the desecration and sacrilege; the martyrdom of priests is common in Church history. The most terrible thing was the setting up of a State Church independent of Catholic jurisdiction and under the control of the government. The concept of a *national* church is incompatible with Catholic ecclesiology, it is a denial of essential Catholicity, and however frequently in the past the pragmatism and realistic acceptance of disagreeable political force may have obliged the papacy to suffer lay interference with regular ecclesiastical orders there had never been anything like the Revolutionary French reconstruction of the Church – nothing, that is, except for the passage of events in those countries which had ended up as Protestant. The Civil Constitution of the Clergy, of July 1790, was carried out in the name of King Louis XVI, and with powers that derived from extreme interpretations of the Gallican Articles of 1682. The National Assembly used a vocabulary of justification, furthermore, which was plainly Jansenist.

There were two instalments in the transformation of Catholicism in France. First was radical reform, in the Jansenist-Gallican mode, which ended with a schism between those who accepted the Civil Constitution of the Clergy and those who remained loyal to Roman authority. This stage came to end in November 1790, when the National Assembly passed a decree requiring all clergy to take an oath subjecting themselves to the Constitutional Church. Louis XVI's attempt to prevent a law for the compulsory exile of recalcitrant priests ended with the collapse of the monarchy itself, in August 1792. Many of the lower clergy supported the Assembly's radical reform, since they were only an extension of the Gallican principles with which they had for long been in sympathy. Indeed, a majority of both bishops and priests supported the Civil Constitution of the Clergy, and it was only when the oath required them to choose between allegiance to the pope or to the state that real division appeared among them: only 4 of the 160 bishops took the oath, though a majority of the lower clergy did. Once the issue of the oath slipped from prominence, however, 85 of the bishops adhered to the Constitutional Church. Some of the dissentient clergy were sent to camps in Corsica; many went voluntarily into exile overseas.

The Assembly had begun its reconstruction of the Church with a familiar round of reforms – redistribution of clerical incomes, appropriation of ecclesiastical revenues, abolition of tithes, confiscation of property, dissolution of the religious orders. Then came the Civil Constitution of 1790. Dioceses were reduced in number and the surviving ones were made to correspond not to ancient sees but to the boundaries of civil departments of government. Bishops and priests were to be chosen by electoral committees, and new systems of payment were introduced. In all these changes there was no consultation either with the hierarchy of the French Church or with Rome. Pius VI declared the Civil Constitution schismatic – as, of course, it was.

The next phase of religious reconstruction in France followed the death of the King. This was the attempt at de-Christianization of the state and of society itself. Here the influence of the ideas of the Enlightenment were embodied in Positivistic experiments, and opened up a gap between the urban professional classes, who had made the Revolution, and the rural peasantry, who remained Catholic. The pattern of allegiance was actually very complex, though the Terror operated to drive surviving urban Catholicism underground, especially when the official Constitutional Church started to disintegrate in 1793. The imposition of Positivist new rites, to replace Christianity, at first rather randomly, became systematic in 1793, with the Festival of Reason and state sponsorship of the cult of the 'Supreme Being'. The ideology of the Revolution was Deist; in practice it became exuberantly atheist. Churches were attacked by the mob, the Blessed Sacrament was desecrated, royal and episcopal tombs were opened up and their occupants' remains thrown to the crowds. From Rome the Pope observed what he believed was the inevitable consequence of denying Catholic teaching. In Paris, the Directory remained anti-Christian, and extended the dismantling of the Church to countries under French control – Belgium, Switzerland and the Rhineland. The papal enclave of Avignon was removed from the pope's jurisdiction.

As the Revolution reached Italy its principles were enforced there too. Monasteries and convents were closed, Church property was confiscated. In the Roman Republic, set up by Napoleon's armies in the Holy City itself, the cardinals were exiled or arrested, ecclesiastical dress was prohibited, and art treasures were taken from the papal residences and the city churches and sent to France. Pius VI became a prisoner of the French and was taken to Valence, where he died in 1799.

Napoleon's pragmatism included toleration of the Church – under Gallican conventions – and the Concordat of 1801, made with the new pope, Pius VII, was a realistic acceptance by both parties of some permanent truths. Napoleon recognized that it was impossible to reconstruct human nature and change long-term historical conditioning in a few years of secular substitutes for religion, and the papal Secretary of State, Cardinal Consalvi, realized that the modern nation-state was here to stay. (Napoleon's first act on arriving in exile, ironically, was to attend a civic Mass in the small cathedral of Portoferraio on Elba.) The Concordat described Catholicism as the religion of the majority of the French people; papal approval was given to the rearrangement of the French dioceses, to the state's right to name bishops, and to the grant of official religious tolerance. Pius VII attended Napoleon's self-coronation of 1804 in Notre Dame Cathedral.

Most of the Catholic heartlands of Europe had passed under French control during the Revolutionary wars, so by the time of Napoleon's own

Jacques-Louis David's famous depiction of the coronation of Napoleon in Notre Dame Cathedral in 1804. The Emperor places a crown upon his wife's head, as the Pope and the Archbishop of Paris look on.

final exile in 1815, the organization of the Catholic Church was in ruins. The central bureaucracy in Rome itself was disrupted, the Sacred Congregations unable to get a satisfactory flow of information. In very many places the religious orders had been dispersed, Church property seized, and the clergy left without direction. With so many colleges closed down by the state, the education of new generations of seminarists was interrupted. Rather a dangerous number of the higher clergy had actually defected to the new state Churches. In Germany, the title of Holy Roman Emperor, redolent of the centuries of co-operation between the papacy and the successors of Constantine, was surrendered in 1806, and the three great ecclesiastical Electors were deposed. Everywhere a semblance of Catholic ministry managed to endure, but everywhere an enormous and formidable task of reconstruction lay before the curial officials.

Two features of Catholic reconstruction had lasting side-effects. The first was the restoration of the properties and privileges of the Church in each country. For Catholicism was thereafter tied to the political systems that had restored them: subsequent popes, and especially Gregory XII, were noted

Ultramontanism, with its emphas is on the office of the Supreme Pontiff, its Roman centralization, and focus on sacerdotalism sometimes provoked opposition in the Church, but it came to characterize the leading dynamics of 19th-century Catholicism everywhere. Its spread was assisted by the education of clergy at the national colleges in Rome, where they learned Italianate devotional styles. In England, A.W.N. Pugin drew his inspiration from medieval liturgical use, but this page from his *Glossary of Ecclesiastical Ornament* (1844) nevertheless catches something of the current emphasis on ritual precision.

supporters of monarchy. They were themselves among the monarchs who were restored – to the Temporal Power of the States of the Church in Italy. The second feature was the rise of sacerdotalism in the Church, to become a leading characteristic of nineteenth-century Catholicism. Priests gained over lay influence in local Church affairs. There was an incentive: in many parts of Europe lay Catholics had collaborated with the irregular ecclesiastical arrangements enforced by the Revolutionary and Napoleonic authorities – even more obviously than the remaining lower clergy. The emergence of Ultramontanism was an indication of the new sacerdotalism, even though some of its leading advocates were laymen. Ultramontanism, with its exaltation of the office of the Roman Pontiff, was the nineteenth-century equivalent of the Counter Reformation triumphalism which had succeeded the Protestant upheaval in the sixteenth.

The pope whose long reign of over thirty years encountered the force of nineteenth-century liberalism was also the effective engineer of the modern papacy – not by design, but through his response to the dramatic changes of the European world in his day. Giovanni Mastai-Feretti was elected in 1846 and took the title of Pius IX. His contemporaries initially interpreted him as a man of liberal opinions in social and political (but not in theological) policy, of limited intellect, and of personal warmth. The last of these assessments was certainly true; he was also given to humorous observation. When a party of High Church Anglican clergymen visiting Rome once asked him for his blessing he obliged with the liturgical words used in the blessing of incense at Mass: *Ab illo benedicaris in cuius horore cremaberis* ('May you be blessed by Him in whose honour you shall be burned'). Pius IX's liberalism seemed to be indicated by the amnesty of prisoners at the start of his pontificate, and by his preparedness to concede a constitution for his Roman subjects in 1848. But it was in reality, as soon became evident, not an understanding of liberalism which related to the nineteenth-century secular liberals. It looked back to the paternalistic responsiveness to reform of the eighteenth century; it was concerned with changes in the public utilities and agricultural improvements, not in an extended popular franchise.

As for Pius IX's supposed intellectual inadequacies, there should be considerable reserve. The judgement largely derives from Metternich's summary that the new Pope was 'warm of heart but weak of intellect'. Pius did not have a weak mind, however, but one that was academically unformed. He was not a scholar; his intellectual powers, on the other hand, were impressively able to interpret information and to assemble responses. His slight knowledge of diplomacy was adequately compensated by the skills of Cardinal Giacomo Antonelli, his Secretary of State through almost the whole length of his pontificate. Antonelli stood by him in his darkest hour – the flight to Gaeta to avoid the Roman Revolution of 1848 – and remained with him until his death in 1876, just two years before that of Pius IX himself.

The pontificate coincided with the Italian *Risorgimento*, the campaign of the liberals for a united Italy. Its events deeply affected the Pope's assessment of the threats to Catholicism, because the Temporal Power exercised by the papacy over the States of the Church in Italy involved him directly. He had no choice for another reason. In 1843, a Piedmontese priest, Vincenzo Gioberti, had published *Il Primato Morale e Civile degli Italiani*. It was a manifesto for the unification of Italy as a federation of states presided over by the papacy. The book had a tremendous impact, and Pius IX found himself cast in a political role around which heady expectations were rapidly accumulating. At first his instincts were to fulfil this role; hence the grant of reforms in the Papal States in the year following the start of the pontificate, culminating in the Roman Constitution of 1848. This was a version of constitutional monarchy, drawn up by the cardinals and loosely based on that of Louis Philippe in France. In 1831, however, Giuseppe Mazzini had founded Young Italy, with its quasi-mystical concepts of 'God and the People' quite at vari-

Giacomo Antonelli was Cardinal Secretary of State during almost all of Pius IX's pontificate, and therefore had the extraordinarily difficult task of seeking accommodation of the diverse opinions of the European powers over the Italian question. His guiding principle, however, was the protection of Pius's own adhesion to the Temporal Power of the papacy in the States of the Church. By the time he died in 1876 he had seen the unravelling of nearly all his work.

ance with Pius's understanding of his duties as a constitutional sovereign. The assassination of the papal Prime Minister, Count Pellegrino Rossi, the setting up of a revolutionary Triumvirate in Rome by Mazzinians in 1848, the abolition of the Temporal Power, and the Pope's flight to Gaeta – with its evocation of the horrific events during the Napoleonic Republic – ended any realistic prospect of Gioberti's grand design. The incompatibilities between Pius IX's view of liberalism and the behaviour of the secular liberals who had supported the revolutions of 1848 across Europe had been made searingly evident.

It should be noticed, however, that on his return to Rome in 1850 Pius IX resumed his original reform programme; he had not become, as insisted by later historical interpretation (put together by a new generation of liberals) a reactionary. By the late 1850s the administration of the Papal States was largely in the hands of laymen, and the policies of public works and social improvement, the schools and the hospitals and the railways, were continued. Pius IX did not distinguish between his spiritual and his temporal sovereignty in relation to the papal possessions in Italy. He spoke, indeed, of the 'special character' of his sovereignty. The existence of the States of the Church guaranteed the independence of the leadership of the worldwide Catholic Church from the local ambitions of the secularizing politics of Italian nation-builders.

First among these, in the forces of the *Risorgimento*, was the Kingdom of Piedmont. The Siccardi Laws in Piedmont were intended to assist the creation of a modern liberal state, where there was a separation of Church and State, secular education, and the dissolution of surviving 'medieval' institu-

The assault by European Liberals upon the States of the Church in Italy was consistently resisted by Pius IX, who regarded the Temporal Power as an essential prerogative in preserving papal independence. Vincenzo Gioberti had argued for an Italy united under the presidency of the Holy See in 1843, and the dream lingered of a peaceful solution to the issues raised by the *Risorgimento*. In this popular print of the 1860s, Pius IX, King Victor Emanuel II of Piedmont and Giuseppe Garibaldi are shown in unlikely accord.

tions such as the monasteries. Hence the *Law of the Convents* in 1855, which was intended to disband most of the religious houses. The officials of the curia in Rome had, of course, seen all this before; it was the old policy of Jansenism and Gallicanism in an Italian context. Wherever the liberals were successful in Italy the secularizing laws were extended – as in fact they were to the Papal States themselves, and to the city of Rome, after their final seizure from the Church in 1870.

The anti-clerical policies of the Italian liberals explain the anti-liberal pronouncements that came to define Pius IX's pontificate, as the world judged it. Where the European liberals beheld the march of intellect and social progress, the papal administration recognized only the spoliation of ecclesiastical institutions. The papacy, concerned primarily with universal truths and eternal principles, discerned grave philosophical errors in what to the temper of enlightened European opinion seemed to be the sacral values of modernity. There was a complete mismatch of world views, no shared vocabulary of social existence. And so there was never any possibility that when Rome compiled a catalogue of the wrong ideas of the age, drawn from recent papal declarations, there could be any meeting of minds. It was, as Antonelli expressed it in his Introduction to the *Syllabus of Errors* of 1864, 'a most unhappy age'. The list of eighty condemned propositions seemed to be an assault upon the nineteenth century, culminating, as it did, in the rejection of the maxim *Romanus Pontifex potest ac debet cum progressu, cum liberalismo et cum recenti civilitate sese reconciliare et componere* ('The Roman Pontiff can and should reconcile and harmonize himself with progress, with liberalism, and with recent civilization'). The secular liberals were confirmed in their belief that the Catholic religion was irredeemably hostile to progress, Gioberti's programme for an Italian federation under the

pope finally expired, and the school of Liberal Catholicism experienced, not for the first time, shocked disillusionment.

The Liberal Catholics have featured prominently in accounts of nineteenth-century Catholicism written by later Catholic theologians and by Protestants. Yet their influence on the institutional Church was not great, nor did they form anything like a coherent intellectual movement. But intellectuals writing about intellectuals of the past generally tend to exaggerate their significance in the movement of events, and the Liberal Catholics have borne much weight as evidence of the intransigence of Rome. Earlier Liberal Catholics, such as the Abbé de Lamennais and Henri Lacordaire, the writers of *L'Avenir* in France, were concerned with reconciling Catholicism with popular political movements, and with issues of personal liberty, in the 1830s. The politics they envisaged were not all that popular, and amounted to versions of bourgeois liberalism. They were received, however, by excited sympathizers, as being extremely advanced. Their inclinations were condemned in the Encyclical *Mirari Vos*, in 1832, for constituting a programme for the separation of Church and State and for Indifferentism (relativism) in religion. The second generation of Liberal Catholics articulated a higher polemicism and were more moralistic. When stripped to essentials their policies for the reform of the Church were not dissimilar, however. At the Malines Conference in 1863 Charles de Montalembert argued for 'a free Church in a free State' – the old slogan of the Mazzinians. At Munich, in the same year, Ignaz von Döllinger uttered grand principles supposedly taught by history, science and reason. Lord Acton, the leading British Liberal Catholic at the time, and a pupil of Döllinger, espoused views on the historical frailty of papal claims, which led to an indirect curial censure of his *Home and Foreign Review*. Montalembert did manage to vent his displeasure with the high-minded tone of British foreign policy – which consistently supported the Italian Liberals, and so undermined the papacy, while simultaneously endorsing the Sultan's oppressive rule in Constantinople.

Some of the earlier Liberal Catholics had also been Ultramontanists, yet the influence of Liberal Catholicism, in a diluted form, may nevertheless be discerned in the opposition to Ultramontanism which surfaced among the 'Inopportunists' at the Vatican Council of 1869–70. Ultramontanism itself was not a 'movement', any more than Liberal Catholicism was. It was a prevalent ethos, a practical summation of the centralizing tendencies of the nineteenth-century curia, a party label in the divergences of view over Catholic order throughout the world. The publication of Joseph de Maistre's *Du Pape* in 1819 provided an ideological pedigree, and had the effect of encouraging papal authority as part of a revived emphasis on legitimacy which prevailed in the atmosphere of restoration following the fall of Napoleon. François de Chateaubriand's *Génie du Christianisme*, of 1802,

Lord Acton, doyen of the Liberal Catholic writers of the mid-19th century, and Regius Professor of Modern History in the University of Cambridge from 1895. He was consistently regarded as unsound by Rome – not unreasonably, in view of his systematic subversion of the historical claims of the papacy.

which had attracted a kind of cult following, was a rejection of rationalism; it exalted traditional, and therefore papal, understandings of faith and practice. By the time of the Vatican Council it was an Ultramontane publicist, Louis Veuillot, and his paper *L'Univers*, which had the ear of Pius IX. The Pope himself took an active part in the foundation of the Jesuit journal *Civiltà Cattolica*, published in Rome, which set out to counter anti-Ultramontane journalism.

In the confrontation of Liberal Catholicism and Ultramontanism – in relation to social and political issues – the latter won the day in the Church, but in most countries most Catholics were probably untouched by the distinctions drawn by the literary combatants, and were loyal to the pope and hostile to the forces of the *Risorgimento* because that is what by instinct they knew to be right. And they were informed about affairs in Italy. The press of western Europe and North America was overwhelmingly supportive of the Italian liberals and clamoured – as Garibaldi's sensational visit to England showed in 1864 – to denounce the Temporal Power of the pope as an embodiment of every species of political evil.

BELOW In 1917, the Virgin, who identified herself as Our Lady of the Rosary, appeared to three children at Fatima in central Portugal. She delivered a number of messages relating to the devotional life and to turmoil in the world (the First World War was still being fought). This photograph of the three children was taken shortly after the first apparition. The basilica at Fatima is visited by enormous numbers of pilgrims.

The elevation of papal authority under Pius IX produced some of the most important Catholic statements of modern times, and two dogmatic definitions. To appreciate the circumstances of the proclamation of the doctrine of the Immaculate Conception of the Virgin, in 1854, it is necessary to recognize the growth of popular devotions, and of popular preaching and parochial missions. By the middle of the century the cult of the Virgin, and rosary devotions, pervaded Catholic religiosity. A miraculous apparition of the Virgin had appeared at La Salette in France, in 1846; in 1858 she appeared to Bernadette Soubirous in the grotto at Lourdes. The proclamation of the Immaculate Conception is part of the atmosphere of heightened Marian devotion. The doctrine itself had been widely believed in the Early Church, and in 1476 Pope Sixtus IV had approved a Feast in honour of the Immaculate Conception. In 1848, Pius IX appointed a commission of theologians to examine the doctrine, and consulted the bishops of the world – who were virtually all in favour of a dogmatic definition. A draft was prepared by Giovanni Perrone, the leading Jesuit theologian in Rome, and a proclamation was issued in December 1854. The Pope had acted on his own inherent authority; there was no procedure of definition through a General Council. In Rome a slender column was set up in the Piazza di Spagna in honour of the Virgin Immaculate: it has been garlanded by the pope each December, to the present time. Pius IX had demonstrated an important papal prerogative in the definition; it showed that dogmatic articles of faith did not require the approval of a Council. In 1950, when Pope Pius XII

RIGHT In 1858, a peasant girl, Bernadette Soubirous, received visions of Our Lady of the Immaculate Conception – the doctrine had been formally proclaimed, after centuries of belief, in 1854 – in a grotto at Lourdes in the French Pyrenees. In 1862, the visions were recognized by the Church, following miraculous healings at the grotto. Lourdes remains one of the world's great Marian shrines. This photograph from the 1970s shows the sick hearing Mass outside the grotto.

ABOVE The bishops from throughout the world assembled in Rome, at St Peter's Basilica, for the First Vatican Council (1869–70). It was the first Council to be called since Trent in the 16th century; its work was suspended when war broke out between France and Prussia, and the armed forces of the Piedmont invaded and occupied the city of Rome.

proclaimed the dogma of the Assumption of the Virgin, there was, again, consultation with the bishops but no procedure through a Council. That, too, was a doctrine which had always been believed since the earliest traditions. Over the doctrine of Papal Infallibility, however, Pius IX was reluctant to proceed in a matter so close to his own person without conciliar approval.

For the first time since Trent the bishops of the world assembled in General Council at the Vatican towards the end of 1869. Preceding consultations had assured the curia that almost all of the bishops favoured a Council to take general stock of the Church, and preparatory commissions had established an agenda – the two *schemata*, on the nature of the Faith, and on the relationship between Church and State. Historical interpretation has often followed the suspicions of national governments at the time in imagining that the Council was intended to authenticate, with the sanction of the bishops, the contents of the *Syllabus of Errors*, and to enthrone the triumph of Ultramontanism. This reading of events is a distortion. Certainly the Ultramontane parties were successful to the extent that the doctrine of Papal Infallibility was their intended goal at the Council. But Infallibility was not on the agenda of the Council, and it does not appear to have been, at least initially, informally promoted by the Pope himself behind the scenes. The *Syllabus* (not itself an infallible pronouncement) necessarily concerned itself with the alien ideologies that appeared to threaten Catholicism, and these were to form the substance of the first *schema* before the Council; again, however, the Council was not called to legitimize the *Syllabus* – it simply indicated that the issues of the day implied broad and theoretical questions which any consideration of the nature of the Church would inevitably raise. The long reign of Pius IX meant that most of the cardinals were his own appointments, and this naturally assisted a certain homogeneity of opinion.

Most accounts of the proceedings are preoccupied with the definition of Infallibility, and this actually ignores the importance of its decrees on the nature of the Faith and the dangers of philosophical materialism annexed to nineteenth-century liberalism and socialism. It was the bishops who insisted on pressing the matter of Infallibility. When they did, however, they found Pius IX exceedingly willing to open the door. 'Before I was Pope I believed in the Infallibility,' he then said, 'now I feel it.' In Rome, the follow-ers of Veuillot, and the English Cardinal Manning, who was a sort of leader of the 'Infallibilists', encouraged him. The *schema* on the nature of the Faith, which became the Constitution *Dei Filius*, was concerned with the relation-ship of faith and reason, and expressed the nature of the Divine Revelation in language appropriate to modern understanding. It was a statement of the substance of Christianity, its exclusivity, its authority and its missionary purpose. The debates elicited no significant differences of interpretation or emphasis. It was the main work of the Council.

The second *schema*, *De Ecclesia*, was intended as a consideration of the pressing issues of Church and State, the spiritual nature of the primacy of the pontiff, and the Temporal Power over the States of the Church in Italy. In the event, these issues were never discussed, since the addition of Infallibility preoccupied the whole time of the session. Those bishops who were opposed to a definition were not hostile to the doctrine of Infallibility as such. They believed, as they declared in the debate, that in the existing climate of opinion the non-Catholic world was unready to understand it; that enemies of the Church would seize upon the definition as a sign that Catholicism was as unprogressive and 'medieval' as they had always insisted. In this conclusion the 'Inopportunists', supported by many Liberal Catholics, were proved right. But the doctrine itself, as nearly everyone contended,

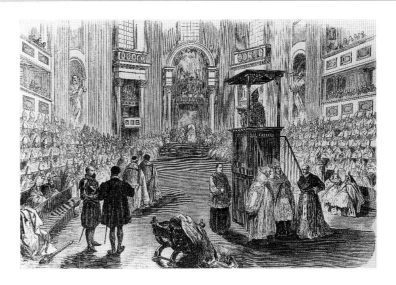

The dogma of Papal Infallibility is proclaimed in St Peter's, 1870.

was essential to Catholic ecclesiology and had always been inherent in the operation of the *consensus fidelium*. It was Christ who had said that the Holy Spirit would protect his followers in truth; and, as his body in the world, the Church – which was in consequence itself holy – was indefectible in the essentials of faith and morals.

Past disputes had derived from uncertainties about identifying the procedure for the pope to speak ex cathedra, from his chair of teaching, and so to certify which pronouncements were infallible and which were not. Some had believed that *only* a general council could provide the occasion. Some others denied the concept of infallible teaching in an institutional sense at all, and located it instead in exclusive resort to Scripture. These had gone off into Protestantism. The Vatican Council sought to define how infallibility operated in the *magisterium*, the teaching office of the Church, and in the office of the papacy as its intrinsic authenticator. The successor of St Peter, whom the Lord himself commanded to teach his flock, had intrinsic authority in the declaration of doctrine. This was not an effect that attached to mere opinions of the pope, or to instructions of office, or policy, but was resident in solemn declarations made ex cathedra. The Immaculate Conception showed the process at work in 1854.

Only extreme papalists, like some of the Veuillotists, spoke as if virtually every utterance of the pope was infallible. Their assertions, however, were picked up in Protestant polemicism. As it turned out, the 'Inopportunists' numbered eighty-eight in the last vote of the General Congregation, and in the formal and final vote 533 voted *placet*, and only two voted *non-placet*. St Peter's basilica darkened as a thunderstorm descended upon the final proceedings, obliging attendants to bring on more lighted tapers in order to determine the outcome. Papal Infallibility became a dogma of the Church, an article of faith, in the Constitution *Pastor Aeternus* in July 1870. What anyway

had been believed for centuries, and had been upheld against the advocates of conciliarist ecclesiology, what had been preached by Ultramontanes and had divided the Catholic Liberals, and what had confirmed the Protestants in their supposition that 'Popery' was a tissue of superstition, now became, as Catholics believe, a guarantee of Christian truth.

By an unhappy chance, the troops of Piedmont occupied Rome a week later, and the Council was adjourned. The *Risorgimento*, as well as Catholic orthodoxy, therefore triumphed simultaneously. To the surprise of the exultant European liberals there was no popular rejoicing or cheering reception for the liberating troops in the city. Pius retired to the Vatican itself with his Swiss Guards, and the Quirinal Palace was taken over by the liberal politicians. The priests wisely adopted what is today called a low profile. Ferdinand Gregorovius (an unsympathetic German observer) noticed that 'the cardinals never show themselves, or if they drive out, their carriages bear no marks of distinction; all their pomp and magnificence have ended in smoke.'

The European Powers had not favoured intervention at the Council (though some had thought of it) – the Catholic heads of government had not been invited as at preceding councils. Now some governments offered the

Pope refuge in their territories. He declined. But in the midst of the debris of papal Rome it was at least clear that the Vatican Council had itself been successful. Most of the 'Inopportunists' worldwide had submitted to the definition of Infallibility – a significant dissenter was Döllinger, who was excommunicated in 1876. Bishop Félix Dupanloup of Orléans, a prominent 'Inopportunist', accepted the doctrine. So, in England, did John Henry Newman, perhaps the greatest Catholic in the English-speaking world of the nineteenth century. He is difficult to categorize theologically, but had written all his life against liberalism in religion; and although he was suspected of unsoundness in some quarters in Rome, and had reservations about the wisdom of the formal declaration of Infallibility, he quietly accepted the will of the Church.

So it was a united Church that Pius IX ruled from the loneliness of his last years within the Vatican – which he never left again. In November 1870, the Piedmontese state imposed a settlement. By the Law of Guarantees, to which the Pope declined to be a party (and so it never became a treaty) the pope was recognized as a sovereign in his own right, the papacy was conceded the Vatican, the Lateran, and the summer residence at Castel Gandolfo. The Temporal Power had thus contracted to three properties, and even these were to be owned by the Italian state and merely reserved to the exclusive use of the pontiff. This arrangement lasted until superseded by the more generous terms of the Lateran Treaty of 1929.

Pius IX's last years were also troubled by a resurgence of anti-clerical secularism, this time in Germany. Bismarck's initiation of what became known as the *Kulturkampf* was a familiar enough sequence of assaults upon the independence of the Catholic Church in Prussia. It was not inspired, however, by distaste for the Vatican Council of the sort that sent Gladstone in England rushing to the desk of polemicism. The *Kulturkampf* was a dimension of Bismarck's conception of the omnicompetence of the modern state, and was to that extent familiar enough. The May Laws of 1872 attempted to subject the Church to an Ecclesiastical Court appointed by the state – a largely Lutheran state, at that. All candidates for the priesthood were required to be educated in state institutions; civil marriage was to replace marriage in church. Eleven bishops were imprisoned in 1874 for failure to comply, and in the following year the Vatican condemned the Laws in the Encyclical *Quod Nunquam*. The anti-clerical code was reproduced in Austria, Belgium and Switzerland.

In the world beyond Europe secularism also provoked tensions, often extreme, in the nineteenth century. In Latin America the eighteenth century Bourbon reforms of the Spanish monarchy, and the Marquis de Pombal's reform of the Brazilian Catholic Church, had included high levels of state interference with the internal operations of the Church, but they were acceptable to the local bishops who anyway shared the essential values of the Iberian monarchies and were accustomed to state intervention. When the Spanish colonies revolted against Spain early in the nineteenth century the independent republics everywhere continued to control and regulate the Catholic Church as a natural part of the Hispanic inheritance; in the exercise of ecclesiastical patronage, the old *real patronato*, they claimed the rights formerly attached to the Crown. Periodically, and almost everywhere, the new states fell into the hands of secularist liberals and radicals, many of whom, like Benito Juárez in Mexico, armed with the Ley Lerdo of 1856, explicitly sought the destruction of the social influence of the priests in order to create, as the liberals supposed, an enlightened and progressive society.

It was an extraordinary paradox that the republics all preserved constitutional connections between the Catholic Church and the state – and then, at various times, used the relationship to assail or even abolish the very existence of ecclesiastical institutions. In what became a parallel to European upheaval, but in a rather more violent manner, there were all the usual policies: the dissolution of the religious orders, the confiscation of Church property, the secularization of education, and eventually, in most places, formal disestablishment. An unexpected stimulus was provided between 1820 and 1823 when a liberal government in Spain itself introduced secularizing legislation.

In Latin America the pattern was uneven, the assaults episodic rather than sustained. There were decades, in some republics, when Church and State co-existed in relative tranquillity. The Catholic presence in Latin America is now the largest in the world. To a great extent this is explained by early successful indigenization, and in part by the pragmatism of the papacy – anxious, in the first years of the republics, to avoid the setting up of schismatic Churches by disaffected regimes.

In the Philippines, where there is also a vibrant and important Catholic Church, the separation of Church and State was arranged peacefully as a constitutional requirement of the cession of the country to the United States in 1898. In America itself a small Catholic population had accepted the Revolution against the British Crown, but were inactive. Like society in general, they came to regard the separation of Church and State, in the First Amendment to the Federal Constitution of 1787, as an essential ingredient of liberty. With the huge immigrations of the nineteenth century, especially from Ireland, Germany, Italy and Poland, and in the twentieth century from Latin America, the Catholic Church became the largest single denomination in the United States. Its integration with the prevalent social and moral values, which in America had a sacral quality, was so complete that it prompted warnings from Rome: Leo XIII condemned departure from Catholic regularity under the title of 'Americanism'. More damaging, since it

LEFT The Irish in New York have always celebrated St Patrick's Day with vigour, in honour of Ireland's patron saint. Here, the procession of 1999 passes St Patrick's Cathedral. Italian Catholics in the city hold a comparable street celebration to mark St Januarius's Day: the patron of Naples.

ABOVE RIGHT Elizabeth Ann Seton – 'Mother Seton' – who helped to establish Catholic schools in the United States, starting with a girls' school in Baltimore. She also founded the first free Catholic schools at Emmitsburg, Maryland after her move there in 1809. The Catholic parochial educational network grew in the 1850s to make provision for those conscientiously unable to accept the non-denominational religious instruction in the public schools. Mother Seton also established the American Sisters of Charity. She died in 1821 and was canonized in 1975.

initiated local conflicts, was use by Catholic parishes of lay trusts to secure ecclesiastical property. Decrees against the practice, which appeared to emulate Protestant custom, were issued by the First Plenary Council of the Catholic Church in the United States in 1853.

Everywhere in the world modern developments in education have furnished occasions of division between the Catholic Church and government. For Catholics the nature of education is not a matter of professional or personal formation merely: it is about the presentation of knowledge in a spiritual culture that will help to determine the eternal welfare of souls. Catholic separate education in America resulted from developments in the evolving public schools in the mid-nineteenth century. At the Third Plenary Council in 1884 the bishops adopted a national educational policy, with

Anti-Catholic rioting and 'No-Popery' literature were a feature of popular culture in Britain, America and Canada in the mid-19th century. In the United States, militant Protestantism combined with Nativism in the 'Know Nothing' political parties, which in the 1850s achieved considerable electoral success in a number of states. In the notorious Philadelphia riots of 1844 forty people were killed in three days of disturbances.

separate Catholic schools and colleges, which was later approved by Rome. The public schools were by then teaching a non-denominational version of Christianity at variance, as the bishops contended, with Catholic truth. It was, indeed, a practical indoctrination of the very Indifferentism condemned in the *Syllabus of Errors*.

Widespread anti-Catholic rioting in the mid-century – a hundred were killed in one riot alone at Louisville in 1855 – indicated to the bishops that the environment was not benign. There were 'No Popery' riots in Canada, too, in the same years. In Canada, however, the relations of Church and State did not have a similar course over education, since there the Catholics, in all the provinces, received government grants in support of their separate schools. In the United States the public schools eventually secularized as a result of strict interpretation of the constitutional separation of Church and State, so that since the mid-twentieth century no religious observances or teaching have been allowed in public schools at all. In Canada, on the other hand, the Catholic Church received a share of the funds raised by the secularization of the Clergy Reserves in 1854, and still receives government funding for its educational work. In South Africa, the Catholics were given state support until 1879 in Cape Province, and in the Union of South Africa as a whole their mission schools received state financial aid until 1983. In England, Catholic schools have received state grants since 1847.

As he surveyed the Church from within the Vatican, the ageing Pius IX must have discerned a darkening landscape. The Temporal Power had been lost, the assaults of the secularists had persisted, educated opinion seemed impervious to his warnings about the impending descent of materialist attitudes to human life. And yet the Catholic Church was vigorous and universal – universal in a way it had never been before. His last months were spent planning the restoration of the hierarchy in that most Calvinist of countries, Scotland (achieved a month after his death). Even in Protestant lands, therefore, there were signs of what Newman had famously called the 'second spring'. Pius IX received a personal devotion from all over the world on a scale no pope had before experienced. At his death in February 1878 there was great sadness, and the inevitable sense, after one who had reigned so long, that an era was closing. His tomb was in the church of San Lorenzo Fuori le Mura – the only historic building in Rome, a protected city, to be demolished by a bomb in the Second World War.

Uncertain Frontiers

7

Mother Teresa of Calcutta attends the sick, photographed in 1979. An Albanian Catholic nun, born in 1910, she trained with the Sisters of Loreto in Italy before working among the poor in Ireland and in Bengal. She founded the Missioners of Charity, an Order that received papal recognition in 1950. Her work coincided with the humanist moralism of contemporary western society, and she thus acquired an international reputation in her lifetime. She died in 1997.

'The Catholic Church for decades, and especially in the past ten years,' noted Pius XII in 1956, 'is undergoing one of the most dangerous persecutions she has ever known.' He was referring to actions of the east European Communist governments, in which he correctly recognized a militant enemy of the Catholic view of human life. After the October Revolution of 1917 in Russia, the imposition of east European versions of Marxism following the Second World War, and the victory in China of Mao Tse-tung in 1949, the people of something like half the world had fallen under direct Communist control. The revolutions coincided with great twentieth-century advances in techniques of mass communication, with the development by governments of popular education, and with collectivist procedures by which the modern state progressively intervenes in the lives of citizens.

It was not only in Communist regimes that the aggrandisement of the modern state was beginning to confront the Church with materialist understandings of the nature of human existence. In liberal democracies, too, the ascendancy of collectivism increasingly equipped the state with the means of propagating practices of social association and regulation which, however incoherently rendered in ideological terms, were in their way no less dogmatic – and in their long-term and subtle effects no less totalitarian – than the Marxist states. A new conflict of Christianity and materialism was beginning. By the time of the collapse of European Communism at the end of the 1980s the materialist basis of life in society was well established; expressed in the familiar and seemingly benign practices of welfare collectivism it went largely unperceived. By then the Christian understanding of the unique nature of Revelation, of the inherent sinfulness of humanity, and of the prospects of immortality – all essentials of the Church's teaching – were slipping away from the professions of the state and the consciousness of individuals.

A poster celebrating Pope Leo XIII's Encyclical *Rerum Novarum*, 1891; one of a series of statements in which he promoted the rights of workers, legitimized collective bargaining, and insisted on the necessity of proper housing and sanitary conditions. The style of the poster anticipates Socialist Realist art of the Soviet era.

In this perspective, Pius IX's lost contest with the forces of the *Risorgimento* in the local theatre of Italy was not the end of a sequence but one set of events in a continuing confrontation, as the papacy viewed it, with modern philosophical error – with materialist interpretations of the place of human life in the purposes of the creation. Pius IX had not been opposed to the advances of science or the enlightenment of the mind, but to the secularizing policies of the modern state as embodied in the Italian liberals. Between the *Syllabus of Errors* and the philosophical writings of Pope John Paul II there was a direct connection. Both were concerned with the ways in which modern arrangements of human society subordinated men and women to artefacts of their own creation, whether in terms of ideas or political structures. There was, of course, a shift in the vocabulary and images used by the two pontiffs, but not really in emphasis. Christianity, they believed, had the capacity to liberate humanity from subjection to materialist ideas, for it located the purpose of human life not in the service of the state, nor even of the public, but in acknowledgement of the eternal principles of the divine order made known to men and women by the actual Revelation of God. The enunciation of these principles, expressed appropriately to the understanding of each age and place, constituted the main substance of papal teaching between Pius IX and John Paul II. Thus the encyclicals have a consistent unity.

There has been much commentary by modern historians and theologians on the 'Social Encyclicals' of Leo XIII, and some of them do indeed have a clearly intended social message – *Rerum Novarum* in 1891, for example, urges the importance of reasonable working hours, of sanitary conditions, of wages 'not to be insufficient to support a frugal and well-behaved wage-

Leo XIII, who became Supreme Pontiff in 1878, photographed in 1880. Gioacchino Pecci had been a Vatican diplomat and became familiar with social issues through postings to London, Paris and Cologne. In the Encyclical *Immortale Dei*, he defined the nature of a Christian state in neo-Thomist categories, and both in this and in other pronouncements he emphasized the compatibility of Catholicism and modern democracy.

RIGHT Henry Edward, Cardinal Manning. Like Newman, he was a convert from Anglicanism, and also an Oratorian; unlike Newman, however, who remained in the world of scholarship, Manning was an ecclesiastical administrator (as Archbishop of Westminster from 1865 to 1892), and a close adviser to Pius IX – whose Ultramontane dispositions he shared. His mediation on behalf of the workers in the London Dock Strike of 1889 gave him a popular following. He is shown here in a *Vanity Fair* caricature of 1871.

earner'. It also acknowledged the right of every man to property as a matter of Natural Law. But the Encyclical is mostly about the antecedent rights of the family against the powers of the state: 'the state must not absorb the individual or the family.' The main theme of Leo XIII's encyclicals is the priority and inviolable authority of Natural Law in the foundation of social association; he was concerned with issues that would today be discussed in terms of Human Rights. There were occasional citations of Aquinas, but the understanding of Natural Law in the encyclicals is not really a construction of neo-Thomism; it depended on Natural Law theory as developed by European philosophical thought in the seventeenth and eighteenth centuries, and actually has a strikingly modern application. 'When, therefore, it is established that man's soul is immortal, and endowed with reason, and not bound up with things material, the foundation of natural liberty is at once most firmly laid,' (*Libertas*, 1888). Time and time again the message implicit in Pius IX's struggle with the ideas of the Italian liberals recurs: the *Risorgimento* is seen to be a precursor of universal philosophical assault on Catholic order. 'Modern theories of political power have already been the cause of great evil,' as Leo XIII wrote in *Diuturnum* (1881) 'and it is to be feared lest in the future these evils shall reach the worst extremes.' Events in the twentieth century bore out his predictions.

The 'Social Encyclicals' of Leo XIII and Pius XI were frequently referred to as an authority by the hierarchies of many countries both at the time of their issue and subsequently. They do, indeed, amount to a very considerable body of teaching. Pius XI actually reproduced the ancient claim to allow the right of rebellion against unjust rulers, 'when the state invades liberty and violates justice'. The words came from his *Apostolic Letter to the Mexican Bishops* of 1937, and refer to the persecution of the Church under Lázaro Cárdenas. There was a strong social motivation in the assault upon Catholicism inspired by Marxist ideology (as in the case of Mexico) which should

feature prominently in any assessment of the conditions that helped to define Catholic social teaching.

In general, however, the social teaching of the Church has in the twentieth century been formulated in relation to the liberal democracies and has not usually involved conflict with the state. In Australia, for example, Archbishop Daniel Mannix of Melbourne, who died in 1963, had originally achieved notice (and notoriety) for opposition to conscription in the First World War. Many Australian Catholics were of Irish descent and (as in the United States) this gave Mannix and the Australian hierarchy an incentive to support critiques of British government policy in relation to the Irish question. But in general he supported the broad lines of Australian social and political development, seeking to present a public Catholic commentary but not with hostile intention. Hence the annual *Social Justice Statements* which the Australian bishops published after 1940. Cardinal Henry Edward Manning, in England, had established a long-remembered tradition of Catholic sympathy for working-class advancement when he mediated in the London Dock Strike of 1889. In this context it is instructive to notice that the Catholic of modern times who received the widest measure of public approval was Mother Teresa of Calcutta, and it was not for her devotion to the traditions of the Church, which was very marked, but for her work among the poor.

There were features of collectivism itself which operated to marginalize the influence of the Church. Many of the social, educational and welfare provisions which had formerly been the exclusive concern of religious institutions were transferred to the state during the twentieth century. In some cases this raised no particular problems for the Catholic Church whose resources for social work, anyway, were incapable of meeting the rising expectations, or the plural nature, of modern society. But sometimes the growth of collectivism, especially where it intruded upon the family, and the increasing pervasiveness of secularism and, in some countries, of unsympathetic political ideology, provoked discord. As yet unperceived by many, the spread of materialist assumptions about the nature of life, arising from non-ideological social habit rather than from explicit ideology, all but overwhelmed western nations by the end of the century. The Christian Churches, and especially the Catholic Church with its more systematic structure of ideas, found themselves excluded from a defined role in the life of modern society, and increasingly simply disappeared from public reference.

Yet overt assaults upon the Church have also been numerous. Anticlerical legislation was resumed in France by Jules Ferry in 1879; in 1901 all religious orders were obliged to register with the state, and in 1905 Catholic schools were closed down. In practice, this negated the Concordat of 1801, and St Pius X duly issued a condemnation in 1906. The Concordat made with the German government in 1933 secured a number of beneficial freedoms for the Church, in some measure removing the remnants of the *Kulturkampf.* But violations began almost at once by Nazi Party officials, and in 1937 the papacy issued a Letter to the German bishops to be read in the churches. *Mit Brennender Sorge* ('With Burning Anxiety') denounced the violations as contrary to Natural Law and to the terms of the Concordat. The Letter, in fact, amounted to a condemnation of Nazi ideology: 'In political life within the state, since it confuses considerations of utility with those of right, it mistakes the basic fact that man as a person possesses God-given rights which must be preserved from all attacks aimed at denying, suppressing, or disregarding them.' The Letter also rejected absolutely the concept of a German National Church.

Since national churches are incompatible with Catholic ecclesiology the inclination of totalitarian governments to encourage them, or even to set them up themselves, had plainly to be resisted. In the twentieth century, there were attempts to create state-sponsored 'national' Catholic Churches in China, Mexico, Cuba and eastern Europe. In the Chinese version, established by the Communists, fifty bishops were named by the state after 1957 – in a kind of oriental atheist Gallicanism. None of them was recognized by Rome.

Some conflicts of Church and State were familiar: the anti-clerical legislation of 1913 in Portugal, which followed the termination of the monarchy, led to the exclusion of religion from the schools and the expulsion of the Papal Nuncio. Some old conflicts, on the other hand, were resolved: in 1929 the Lateran Treaty, negotiated between Cardinal Gasparri and Mussolini, not only recognized and guaranteed the existence of the Vatican State but secured Catholic education and Catholic marriage laws throughout Italy – an unexpected victory over the secular legacy of the *Risorgimento.* But disruption to the Church was commonly expressed through the political regulation of national life demanded by modern governments. Perhaps the most rigorous attempts at the complete extinction of the Catholic Church occurred in the Soviet satellite countries, in Mexico under Calles and Cárdenas, and in Albania under Enver Hoxha when the Communist government closed down all places of worship. Ideological incompatibilities were sometimes mixed with personal considerations.

In Argentina, the administration of General Juan Perón had originally been welcomed by the Catholic hierarchy, in the supposition that his social policy, and the cultivation of organized labour, was in correspondence to papal teaching in the encyclicals and to the ideals of the Corporate State – then being promoted by the Catholic Church. In 1943, Perón reintroduced the teaching of the Catholic religion in the Argentine school system; in 1945, he declared that his social policies were indeed inspired by the encyclicals. But he turned against the Church in 1954, in an attempt to extend the control of the state over institutions generally. Perónista mobs burned down

ABOVE After the loss of the city of Rome in 1870, and the end of the Temporal Power, the Pope became – as was said of Pius IX – a 'prisoner in the Vatican'. Finally, in in the Lateran Treaty of 1929, the Italian state recognized the sovereignty of the Holy Father over the Vatican City, enabling the papacy in turn to recognize the Italian state. Here, Mussolini and Cardinal Gaspari sign the treaty.

OPPOSITE In Argentina, General Juan Perón's earlier support for the Catholic Church was exchanged, in 1954, for hostility. He used populist rhetoric to divert the attention of the masses from social unrest to anti-clericalism. Many historic churches in Buenos Aires were pillaged and burned. In this picture of June 1955 a woman grieves over the wrecking of her local church.

churches in Buenos Aires, and there were extravagant denunciations of the clergy in the press. Perón's moral behaviour did nothing to reassure the Church either. The self-conscious re-invention of Eva Perón as a secular saint scarcely seemed appropriate, nor did Perón's own conduct. Next to the Presidential mansion at Olivos was a girls' school with one of whose pupils the President indulged a passionate attachment certainly incompatible with the teachings of the Church. When his advisers remonstrated because the girl was thirteen Perón was unmoved. 'So what,' he is said to have replied, 'I'm not superstitious.' This and similar episodes cannot have endeared the regime to the Catholic hierarchy.

The mutual antipathy of the Catholic Church and the Communist governments, which reached critical levels during the years of the Cold War, was largely ideological. Catholicism, it is true, sometimes supported markedly conservative regimes, and in some historical circumstances gave actual endorsement to anti-Communist political forces, but this was generally the fruit of strategic positioning rather than of inherent adhesion to the political Right. It was also sometimes the case that anti-socialist governments defined a role for the Catholic Church in circumstances where there had been historical links between Christian leaders and traditional ruling

classes. This was especially true in Latin America and in Spain, under the 'National Security' regimes of the mid-century. Catholic teaching, however, was not hostile to Communism because of its social and economic pro-grammes – the redistribution of wealth, the destruction of class society, the dismantling of capitalism, and so forth – but because of its materialist atheism. Overt attacks on the Church and its institutions made by Communist governments seemed proof enough of the militancy of the atheism, such as the imprisonment of Cardinal Wyszynski in Warsaw, and the lengthy enforced refuge of Cardinal Mindszenty in the American Embassy in Budapest, both in the 1950s.

It was Communist philosophy itself that appeared hostile to religion. The Church envisaged humans as morally frail and liable to corruption, so that political oppression may be expected in virtually any kind of polity. Catholicism discerned an enemy in Communism because of its erroneous doctrines about humanity and human capabilities – its systematic Humanism. In the 1960s, particularly, radical idealism inspired by crises of cultural values in western countries, got up largely by opposition to the war in Vietnam, induced a number of Catholic thinkers to re-examine Marxist philosophical materialism, and especially Marx's early writings. The Church sensed a danger that this revisionism would lessen the clarity with which Communism had been rejected. Hence the official disapproval of 'Liberation Theology', which seemed to authorities in Rome, and to local hierarchies, to be essentially a reinterpretation of the Church's mission in the world, and its representation in the vocabulary of Marxism. It was not controversial to assert that the Church should speak up for the poor, but it was conceived to be dangerous and compromising to assert that its core message was about revolution.

There is, perhaps, no intrinsic incompatibility of Marxist philosophical materialism and the biblical depiction of a Divine Creator who discloses himself through the material nature of his creation, nor between humans as moulded by their perception of material reality and Catholic observation that people are in some large measure conditioned by social structures – and receive a knowledge of spiritual truth when it is represented in the world by earthly embodiments that are susceptible to intellectual analysis and categorization. The doctrine of the Incarnation itself is all about the universal becoming mate-rial. But Catholicism is insistent on human transcendence, and completely rejects materialism when materialists themselves insist that the world of material reality is self-explanatory, and so vitiates the sovereignty of God.

In the political arrangements of the modern world the Church has, in its teachings, warned the faithful about wrong views of human purpose found in Marxism, in capitalism, and in materialist Humanism. In 1949, the Holy Office issued a Decree forbidding Catholics to join the Communist Party in

The social authority of the Catholic Church in eastern European countries was challenged early in the Cold War years by the Communist governments, and led to a series of state trials of prominent clergy. In Hungary, Cardinal Josef Mindszenty took refuge in the American Embassy in Budapest – he is seen here on the balcony in November 1956 – an event that drew the world's attention to the sufferings of the Church under the new regimes.

any country, and warning that anyone who did would be excommunicated. The reason given was the materialist atheism of Communism. There had been a stream of encyclicals which had, however, also attacked capitalism, as dependent upon economic and social structures that deny the essential transcendence of humanity. In 1943, Pius XII declared 'the worker, in his efforts to improve his condition, finds himself confronted by a system which, far from being conformable with nature, is contrary to the order established by God, and to the purpose which he has assigned to earthly goods.' There were many Catholic writers, especially, in the 1930s, who assailed capitalism for its baneful effects on the individual person and on social purpose.

The papacy, which remained neutral in both the World Wars of the twentieth century – since it regarded the pastoral care of its adherents as a priority in every country – was nevertheless not neutral in its ideological declarations. It avoided, as was its custom in modern times, directly identifying particular embodiments of wrong ideas in national terms, and condemned them in general language which had, however, very clear applications in the context of the times. This was true in its treatment of Communism, excoriating the Party in universal condemnation rather than country by country. In his Christmas broadcast for 1942 this convention was applied in reference to Germany. Pius XII then spoke of Human Rights in a manner that could only have referred to Nazi policy, and was taken as such at the time. He spoke of 'hundreds of thousands who, without any fault of their own, sometimes only by reason of their nationality or race, are marked down for death or progressive extinction.' The Nazi Party had anyway always embraced neo-pagan ideas. When it had the opportunity, as in occupied France, there was a mass destruction of roadside crucifixes.

As the Catholic social and political teaching which developed after the *Syllabus* of 1864 came, therefore, to reject several versions of materialist views of human life, it might have been expected that it would, Anglican-style, attempt some kind of middle-ground compromise. It did not do so. Instead the Church sought to identify essentially Christian truths about the nature of human life itself, which had universal application, and could be applied sympathetically in differing political societies. This, in the 1930s and 1940s, resulted in the endorsement of the Corporate State. Because this had the misfortune to be most readily aired in nations that opted for Fascism, as in Spain and Portugal, Italy and Latin America, it has sometimes been assumed that mid-century Catholic social teaching had a kind of natural affinity with Fascist politics. This was scarcely the case, however: what it did have was a romantic attachment to a half-mythical understanding of a medieval Catholic ideal of social harmony and integration – before capitalism divided people into horizontal social classes, and the materialism of systematic socialism robbed them of their souls.

Pope Pius XII at his coronation in 1939. Until the pontificate of Paul VI (1963–78) the popes were carried in procession seated in the *Sedia Gestatoria*: a convention going back to ancient Roman custom when the priests were raised in this manner on festal occasions. Pius XII reigned until 1958, steering the Church through the war years by seeking pastoral priorities and maintaining Catholic teaching on the rights possessed by men and women that are independent of the state.

The Encyclical *Quadragesimo Anno*, issued by Pius XI in 1931, accepted the necessity, in modern conditions, of aspects of collectivism; 'owing to changed circumstances much that was formerly done by small groups can today only be done by large associations.' Yet smaller groups within the life of the state still had functions that the state must protect. The letter then outlined a vision: 'The aim of social policy must therefore be the re-establishment of vocational groups.' These bodies would recognize 'the human dignity of the working man,' and end the 'fierce combat' between employers and workers implicit in capitalism. Vocational groups would claim the allegiance of men 'not according to the position they occupy in the labour market, but according to the diverse functions which they exercise in society'. Quotations from Aquinas followed. Here was a species of arts-and-crafts polity that owed inspiration not to twentieth-century Fascism but to medieval guilds. It is easy to see, on the other hand, how readily it could find accommodation with the social beliefs of Mussolini in Italy, with Franco's Spain, and Salazar's Portugal. In Spain, the Church was unavoidably going to side with the Nationalists in the Civil War – which ended with Franco's occupation of Madrid in 1939 – since the Communists and Anarchists had ransacked the churches and killed the priests. Hispanic traditionalism seemed a better prospect than Marxist atheism.

The Liberation Theology of the 1960s appeared to offer a quite different aspect of Marxism. It grew out of sympathy for working-class movements in

The Spanish Civil War, which ended with Franco's occupation of Madrid in 1939, was an ideological *Vorspiel* for the greater European conflict that followed it. Quite apart from historical and class sympathies that the Catholic hierarchy in Spain had with the Nationalists, they were additionally driven into a general support of Franco by the murder of clergy and the burning of churches, carried out by the Communists and Anarchists. Franco's troops are here shown at Mass on the steps of San Nicolas Church in Bilbao.

the cities of Latin America, and for racial equality in Southern Africa. It was actually the work of urban elites, whose radical enthusiasms envisaged the social transformation of the poor. The poor themselves, unable to recognize their own best interests through their false-consciousness (in classic Marxist presentation) were to be re-educated ('conscientization') to recognize their own revolutionary virtue. The most widely read leader of Liberation Theology was the Peruvian priest Gustavo Gutiérrez: his linear message, expressed in Marxist language, was a call to identify the Christian Gospel with the political aspirations of the oppressed classes of Latin America. In this version of *social-cristianismo* the agenda of change was determined by the poor themselves; in reality it was presented by Marxist intellectuals many of whom were actually from Europe and North America. The shortage of Catholic priests throughout Latin America had for some decades necessitated overseas recruitment, and in the heady atmosphere of campus radicalism in the 1960s the priests arrived with Marxist analysis in their backpacks.

The idealism of the times was additionally generated by the revolution in Cuba under Fidel Castro – who had begun by expelling the foreign priests. Castro's tight Communist republic was met by Vatican diplomatic flexibility. Mgr. Cesare Zacchi, the Papal Nuncio in Havana after 1960, even went so far as to suggest that Castro was, 'from an ethical point of view', a Christian. In Chile, similarly, the election to the presidency of the Marxist Salvador Allende in 1970 could be interpreted, as it was by Cardinal Silva Henríquez,

A IGREJA DO MARANHÃO REZA E JEJUA PELA PAZ E JUSTIÇA NO CAMPO

Radicalized interpretations of Catholic teaching existed in many parts of the developing world after the 1960s, but were especially associated with Latin America – perhaps because of the large number of foreign priests, from Europe and North America, who served there. Beneath a banner advocating direct action to help the poor and the oppressed a Mass is offered in Bacabal in Brazil in July 1986.

as a benign development: 'socialism has enormous Christian values which in many ways make it superior to capitalism.' Passages in some of the papal encyclicals could well be cited, if not exactly in support of this assessment, at least not unsympathetically.

But Liberation Theology itself was different. It was a systematic portrayal of Marxism as the authentic application of the Gospel, and as a political alliance between Catholicism and the forces of revolution. Its heroes were such as Camilo Torres, the Colombian priest who had actually joined the Marxist guerrilla fighters, and was portrayed as a sanctified Che Guevara. It is arguable that Liberation Theology was more influential among Left-wing students in western universities than it was on the streets of Latin American cities – but then it never claimed that the poor whose elevation seemed so imminent were articulate. Their proletarian wisdom derived from the *praxis* of the streets; their salvation lay beyond the barricades rather than before the altar. Christianity was practical. The Kingdom of Heaven could be set up in the real world of the present.

Most Catholics in Latin America were probably untouched by the idealistic rhetoric, yet the bishops, in conference, reflected some of its radicalism. They were certainly not all unreconstructed conservatives – very much not, as the resolutions of the first two Conferences of Latin American Bishops indicated. At Medellín in 1968 there was a general disposition to recognize that the Church was on the side of the poor, with an affirmation of some of

the political implications. The public display of such radicalism alarmed Rome – it was not so much the sentiments which disturbed the curial officials as the Marxist social categories used in the bishops' analyses. Pope John Paul II therefore himself addressed the Third General Conference, at Puebla, in 1979. He was clearly critical of some aspects of Liberation Theology which depended, he insisted, on erroneous 're-readings of the Gospel as a result of theoretical speculation rather than authentic meditation on the word of God'. Gutiérrez promptly announced that he and the radicalized theologians had not been criticized since, as he put it, 'we have done no re-readings'. The Pope was alarmed not by the socialism of the Latin American Catholic thinkers but by the secular ideals inseparable, as he saw it, from identifying the message of the Gospel with Marxist revolution. The essential teaching of the Catholic Church (rather than its necessary applications) was concerned with the universal and eternal principles that govern a rightly ordered society, not with the minor issues, even when just, of material distribution.

Since the end of the 1970s, and the disappearance of most of the political issues that gave Liberation Theology such a vogue in the west, little is heard among Catholic thinkers about the need for revolutionary change. Marxism itself has diminished in intellectual influence – in a way a decline to be lamented, since the young have lost with it acquaintance with serious philosophical ideas, even if they are, from a Catholic point of view, wrong ones. There was a paradox at the centre of Liberation Theology. When all the rhetorical clamour about the poor is stripped away it can be seen as a call to use the power of the state, political power, purged as an instrument of bourgeois class interests, as a means of fulfilling the demands of the Gospel in creating social righteousness. It represented, to that extent, a kind of neo-Christendom model, a return to the pre-modern notion of establishing a Christian society through the coercive machinery of political management.

The emancipation of scholarship and learning from the control of the Church, which is one of the most significant ingredients of the modern world, had always necessarily raised problems for the *magisterium*, the teaching office of the Church. The Ultramontane character of the nineteenth-century papacy had sharpened distinctions between orthodoxy and the liability to error, and the century had seen a number of cases – much publicly regretted by Liberal Catholics – in which the curia had censured the purveyors of unsound views. The twentieth century produced another procession of the condemned, from Alfred Loisy and the 'Modernists' to Karl Rahner, Hans Küng and Yves Congar. The Catholic Church is not against speculative theology and philosophy as such, but it sees itself as collectively entrusted with the duty of maintaining the teaching of Christ – whose body in the world it believes itself to be – as defined by the whole people of God and not by individual thinkers.

The Church claims universality: what is declared in one place as truth must be received as truth everywhere or it cannot, by definition, be authentic. Hence the infallibility intrinsic in the apostolate, and explicit in the ex-cathedra pronouncements of the successors of St Peter. The intellectual pluralism of the modern world, and the obvious dethronement of theology as the 'Queen of the Sciences', pointed to the need for a new consultation of the world's bishops to restate the ancient truths in a manner comprehensible within the social circumstances and the intellectual forces of modern culture. The result was the Second Vatican Council, which opened in October 1962 and closed, at the end of the fourth session, in December 1965.

Pius XII had actually thought of a council. The First Vatican Council had never been formally dissolved: it was adjourned, with Italian troops at the gates of Rome, and with France and Germany at war. Pius XII sought to complete its business, but the work on an agenda, which he initiated, ceased in 1951. He died in 1958, and was succeeded by Angelo Giuseppe Roncalli, a Vatican diplomat, who became Pope John XXIII. As he was known to be a conservative, like his predecessor, it was not to be anticipated that he would inspire a reform programme – and he did not do so. His summoning in 1960 of the first synod of the diocese of Rome (a sort of *Vorspiel* for the Council) and the Council itself two years later, were not intended to stimulate far-reaching changes. His celebrated intention of *aggiornamento* (renewal) was exactly that: his hope, amply fulfilled as it turned out, was to revive clarity of doctrine by removing the accretions of redundant culture. He sought a work of restoration.

The Council has often been seen, especially by the promoters of extensive change, seeking authority for their various enterprises, as in itself the source of all that followed in the 1960s. But the Council was not reformist on all fronts, either under John XXIII or under Paul VI who followed him in 1963. The Council did take place, however, in a decade of crisis in western cultural values; a time of escalating expectations, when the past often seemed burdensome and the future seemed to beckon humanity to new hopes. Many of the changes in Catholic practice attributed by later interpreters to the Council would have occurred anyway, in response to the prevailing inclinations of an era that simultaneously prompted changes in the Protestant Churches too. Some of the changes later popularly attributed to the Council actually preceded it. Pius XII, for example, had encouraged lay participation in the Mass in 1947, as well as evening Masses, and dialogue with non-Catholics on matters of faith. The 3,281 bishops who assembled for the Council in 1962 included many who had expectations of change, but few rendered them in particularly radical terms.

The Council made no new dogmatic definitions, and had no need to do so. The Assumption of the Virgin had been promulgated by an exercise of papal authority in 1950, and there was no agenda for further definitions of doctrine. Nor was there any coherent intellectual mode that either prompted the idea of the Council, and so provided an agenda, or emerged throughout its proceedings. The sessions took place in a world of increasing intellectual pluralism, to which the traditional Thomist categories of formal Catholic learning could refer only very indirectly. But no alternatives were likely to achieve universal assent among the Fathers assembled at the Vatican.

Some spoke of the new vision brought by the bishops of the developing world – an enormous body of opinion at the Council. Yet their voices actually only echoed sentiments of the European and North American Catholic leaders, declaiming their own loss of cultural certainty and having no intellectual system or agreed programme to put in its place. The voices of the developing world turned out to be the voices of westernized elites rather than authentic insights raised up from among the dispossessed. The remarkable thing about the Council was that it was able to produce more or less exactly what it set out to do: a statement of the Catholic faith in modules of understanding intelligible to modern culture yet completely conformable to past tradition – an achievement the more remarkable in view of the incoherence of western culture in the 1960s.

The agenda was organized by Cardinal Léon-Joseph Suenens, who had succeeded Cardinal Van Roey as Archbishop of Malines in 1961. Since he

OPPOSITE The bishops of the world assembled in St Peter's Basilica during the Second Vatican Council in October 1962, with Pope John XXIII presiding.

In 1950, the dogma of the Assumption of the Virgin was proclaimed by Pius XII. It had been a matter of faith since the earliest years of the Church, and is venerated in Byzantine Christianity as the feast of the Dormition. Titian's great *Assumption*, an altarpiece at the Frari Church in Venice, was painted in 1516–18.

was rather given to conveying his opinions to the press, Suenens was taken, by them, to be a spokesman for 'open' views of the Council proceedings, almost as leader of progressive policies. He was subsequently, indeed, to become something of a progressive, and to employ the current youth vocabulary of protest in his various utterances – a disposition that in due course alienated him from the confidence of Paul VI. His work on the Council agenda was measured and seminal, however. It was Suenens who opted for the traditional distinction between *ad intra* matters, on the internal nature of the Church and its doctrines, and which became the substance of the Dogmatic Constitution *Lumen Gentium*, and *ad extra* policy, on the relationship of the Church to the world, which became the Pastoral Constitution *Gaudium et Spes*. It was *Lumen Gentium* that defined the Church as the 'People of God', and which heightened consciousness of collegiality. The laity were incorporated into the conduct of Catholic affairs at local levels, and synods of bishops were in future to be convened by the papacy to institutionalize the consultative process. This in practice meant an abandonment of the Ultramontane mystique that had adhered to papal government.

The Constitution was not in any sense, however, a resuscitation of the old claims of collegiality, to the superiority of the bishops over the universal sovereignty of the papacy; nor was it an encouragement to the concept of national self-identity by individual Church hierarchies. The Doctrine of the Church itself was explicit: 'The universal body made up of the faithful, whom the Holy One has anointed, is incapable of being at fault in itself.' Infallibility was reaffirmed, and the office of the Pontiff, as the earthly head, was stated yet again as the proper order of the Church. The Vatican Council

Cardinal Léon-Joseph Suenens, Archbishop of Malines, pays homage to Paul VI in October 1963. Later the relations between the two men were somewhat strained by Suenens's advocacy of radical democratization of ecclesiastical institutions. In the preparations for the Second Vatican Council he had risen to international prominence. Eventually he became a supporter of Catholic Pentecostalism. He died in 1996.

eventually, in 1994, produced a new *Catechism* – just as the Council of Trent had done. Its composition was entrusted to the coordination of Cardinal Joseph Ratzinger (Benedict XVI after 2005), and its version of the Doctrine of the Church unsurprisingly followed the traditional formulations of the Council: 'This pastoral office of Peter and the other apostles belongs to the Church's very foundation and is continued by the bishops under the primacy of the Pope.'

The Council did not consider ecumenism a priority, and its Constitutions did not suggest any new initiatives beyond conventional courtesies and an openness to exchange views with other religious bodies. It is not differences of liturgical use or ceremony, nor the authority of Scripture, nor the office of ministry, as such, that divide Catholicism from the Protestant Churches, but the Doctrine of the Church itself. And that was restated by the Council in a manner that left little space for any realignment. Catholic teaching on the infallible nature of ecclesiastical authority, and an increasing divergence in moral theology, in the second half of the twentieth century, have if anything sharpened the inherent incompatibilities of Catholicism and Protestantism. The Catholic Church is actually an extremely diverse entity, with very considerable internal differences of opinion; but it is united around its Doctrine of the Church, and this is not negotiable.

In 1968, Cardinal Suenens published *Co-responsibility in the Church*, in which he contended for greater practical collegiality by the papacy, and projected a whole series of requirements for participation by the clergy and laity. The book was widely read and caused something of a sensation. But Suenens actually upheld the ultimate supremacy of the papacy – 'the heart and head of collegiality in action' – and never departed from orthodoxy, even when he became preoccupied, as he later was, with Catholic Charismatic extravagancies.

Another who had taken an influential part in the drafting of the documents for the Council was Karol Wojtyla, Archbishop of Cracow. He was a member of the Commission that produced *Lumen Gentium*, and its insistence on the moral consequences of human sovereignty over nature, and the need for the priority of ethical over material considerations in the pursuit of human development, are evidences of the respect in which his views were received. After the brief pontificate of John Paul I (Albino Luciani) from August to September 1978, Wojtyla followed him as pope in October. John Paul II was widely considered, especially by less than sympathetic liberals, as a figure deeply conditioned by his Polish background, by its traditional conservatism, its Marian devotions and its conflict between the Church and the Communist state. He was, indeed, the first non-Italian pope for almost five hundred years. But it was not a particularly east European traditionalism that he brought to his pontificate. By the time

Cardinal Karol Wojtyla, when Archbishop of Cracow, visits the Church at Nowa Huta during its construction. The building was completed in 1977 and became an iconic symbol of the strength of Catholicism in Communist Poland.

of his election he was widely travelled and was, in his long tenure of office, to travel even more extensively than Paul VI, so acquainting the world, through the medium of television, with a public view of the papacy unavailable to preceding generations.

John Paul II's intellectual writings owed their inspiration almost entirely to the phenomenology and ethical theory of Max Scheler, the Catholic sociologist at the University of Cologne about whose ideas Wojtyla wrote his second doctoral thesis in 1959. This work led to his most important book, published in 1969, *The Acting Person*. In its synthesis of the sociology of knowledge and Catholic ethical theory nearly all of Wojtyla's teachings as pontiff can be discerned – first made prominent in the Encyclical of 1979, *Redemptor Hominis*.

In 1978, Wojtyla ascended the papal throne as John Paul II, and became immediately notable, and loved, for the extent of his overseas travel – seeking to encourage the Catholic mission by emphasizing its universal basis. Here, he is seen administering Holy Communion during a visit to Kinshasa in Zaire in August 1985. This was his twenty-seventh international pastoral journey.

The incomplete view of man available to contemporary scientific and philosophical enquiry, he argued, has resulted in a practical subordination of humanity to the products of its own creation. In concrete terms this meant the limiting effects of materialism, both philosophical and actual. The Communist regimes were, he believed, no worse in this than the capitalist ones; indeed, capitalism was the more culpable because it possessed the greater opportunities for freedom of individual choice. In the Encyclical, therefore, he condemned what he called 'consumer civilization'.

Here, and in later pronouncements, this analysis was applied in relation to sexual morality. Men and women had replaced creative views of human sexuality with utilitarian ones – an amplification of Paul VI's warnings about the effects of artificial birth control in *Humanae Vitae* in 1968. Humans were intended by God to be immortal creatures; human life was capable of transcendence, and yet personal behaviour in modern society increasingly demonstrated the lower nature expressed in the pursuit of security, material welfare and pleasure. It was no surprise, John Paul insisted, that the world was now full of fear. He surveyed a moral culture of faithlessness, personal gratification, sexual irregularity, and the separation of sexuality from serious moral purpose. Human sexuality took its providential characteristics from the sacred means by which the race is perpetuated and children are nurtured in true principles. In reality, it was becoming a leisure activity. The maintenance of Catholic teaching in such matters, which to many interpreters both inside and outside the Church seemed restrictive and old-fashioned, was for John Paul an absolutely vital issue in the emancipation of the person from the thrall of self-destructive materialism. Life was not intended to be defined by the pursuit of sexual encounters, or by remorseless exploitation of hedonism. Far from being a narrow understanding of humanity, he believed, Catholic teaching opened up individual lives to higher purpose. Very many did not listen.

At the Semana Santa (Holy Week) processions in Majorca, as elsewhere in the Latin World, penitents wear pointed headdresses and robes, which are directly descended from the ceremonial garments of the priesthood in ancient Rome.

The twentieth century ended with a gathering sense that Humanist materialism had eclipsed the transcendent views of human life upheld by the Church for centuries. There had actually been, during all that time, quite a number of philosophical and moral views with which the Church had felt able to associate its essential message, but none had subordinated men and women to material processes with the consistency of modern Humanism. The increasingly prevalent materialism is the more accessible because it has no moral label by which it can be popularly detected: it is encountered by men and women as unconscious orientations of life and thought, and often seems as evident inside the Churches as outside them. Liberal Catholics appear to question traditional moral theology on the basis of ethical premises derived from the doctrines of the secular Humanists; lay people seem impatient of clerical advice on moral issues. It is an age in which a massive privatization of religious choice is taking place; individual preferences for emotionally satisfying or morally flexible practices are replacing collective adhesion to religious authority.

In western societies attendance at religious services, and vocations to the priesthood and Christian voluntary associations are declining at a rate very similar to that in the Protestant Churches. Modern education, even in institutions conducted by the Church, is plainly not conducive to recruitment of children to the Faith. Such is the effect of cultural pluralism in modern society. In the developing countries, however, the Catholic Church continues to expand. Some imagine that eventually the extension of education, and the consequences of electronic communication, will produce universal secularization. Yet Islamic revivalism of the present time, which takes place among urban and educated people, indicates that the conventional correlation between modernity and religious decline is not securely established. It all depends on the nature of the values conveyed in educational programmes. Perhaps it is institutional religion, rather than self-selected 'spirituality', that is passing from the scene, at any rate in western society. The book of the future has yet to be written. At present even the concept of spirituality itself has been secularized. 'We are building a dictatorship of relativism that does not recognize anything as definitive, and whose ultimate goal consists solely of one's own desires.' The words are those of Benedict XVI.

OPPOSITE Catholic continuity: Pope Benedict XVI ordains twenty-one new priests at St Peter's in Rome in 2005. Vocations to the priesthood and to the religious orders are declining, but the Church is undismayed: it thinks and plans in terms of centuries.

Further Reading

Aveling, J.C.H., *The Jesuits* (London, 1981)

Bardazzi, Marco, *In the Vineyard of the Lord, The Life, Faith, and Teachings of Joseph Ratzinger, Pope Benedict XVI* (New York, 2005)

Barraclough, Geoffrey, *The Medieval Papacy* (London, 1968)

Bossy, John, *Christianity in the West, 1400–1700* (Oxford, 1985)

Brown, Peter, *The Cult of the Saints* (London, 1981)

Butler, Cuthbert, *Benedictine Monachism* (London, 1919; Cambridge, 1961)

—, *The Vatican Council* (London, 1930)

Catechism of the Catholic Church, English edition (London, 1994)

Chadwick, Henry, *The Early Church* (London, 1967)

Duffy, Eamon, *The Stripping of the Altars: Traditional Religion in England, 1400–1580* (New Haven and London, 1992)

Evennett, H.O., *The Spirit of the Counter-Reformation* (Cambridge, 1968)

Freemantle, Anne (ed.), *The Papal Encyclicals* (New York, 1956)

Frend, W.H.C., *The Rise of Christianity* (London and Philadelphia, 1984)

Grant, Robert M., *Greek Apologists of the Second Century* (London and Philadelphia, 1988)

Hales, E.E.Y., *Pio Nono. A Study in European Politics and Religion in the Nineteenth Century* (London, 1954)

Hastings, Adrian, *African Christianity* (London and New York, 1976)

—, (ed.), *Modern Catholicism. Vatican II and After* (London, 1991)

Hennesey, James, *American Catholics. A History of the Roman Catholic Community in the United States* (New York, 1981)

Hughes, Kathleen, *The Church in Early Irish Society* (London and Ithaca, NY, 1966)

Jones, A.H.M., *Constantine and the Conversion of Europe* (New York 1962; Toronto, 1994)

Kelly, J.N.D., *The Oxford Dictionary of the Popes* (Oxford, 1986)

Latourette, K.S., *A History of the Expansion of Christianity* (London, 1947)

Markus, R.A., *The End of Ancient Christianity* (Cambridge, 1990)

McManners, John, *The French Revolution and the Church* (London, 1969)

Mecham, J. Lloyd, *Church and State in Latin America* (Chapel Hill, North Carolina, 1966)

Momigliano, Arnaldo (ed.), *The Conflict between Paganism and Christianity in the Fourth Century* (Oxford, 1963)

Nash, Ronald H. (ed.), *Liberation Theology* (Milford, Michigan, 1984)

Norman, Edward, *Roman Catholicism in England* (Oxford, 1985, 1986)

O'Carroll, Michael, *Pius XII. Greatness Dishonoured* (Dublin, 1980)

Pollard, John F., *The Vatican and Italian Fascism, 1929–32* (Cambridge, 1985)

Reardon, Bernard M.G. (ed.), *Roman Catholic Modernism* (London, 1970)

Schurhammer, Georg, *Francis Xavier* (Rome, 1973–82, 4 vols)

Southern, R.W., *Western Society and the Church in the Middle Ages* (London, 1970)

Ullmann, Walter, *A Short History of the Papacy in the Middle Ages* (London, 1972)

Vidler, Alec R., *Prophecy and Papacy: A Study of Lamennais, the Church and the Revolution* (London, 1954)

Ware, Timothy, *The Orthodox Church* (London, 1993)

Wheatcroft, Andrew, *Infidels: the Conflict between Christendom and Islam, 638–2002* (London, 2003)

Williams, G. Hunston, *The Mind of John Paul II: Origins of his Thought and Action* (New York, 1981)

Picture Credits

Index